BIGGER than ME

Kara Jackson

ISBN 979-8-89243-836-0 (paperback)
ISBN 979-8-89243-837-7 (digital)

Christian Faith Publishing
832 Park Avenue
Meadville, PA 16335
www.christianfaithpublishing.com

Printed in the United States of America

To my father and mother in the faith, Apostle Johnny L. Magee Jr. and First Lady Lilliette Magee, your obedience to God is the ultimate example of life being **BIGGER than OURSELVES**.

Contents

FOREword

Technically, I met Kara the day she was conceived, but officially on May 26, 1983, our birthday. Yes, she and I were born on the same day to the same parents. Kara is my twin sister. She is just shy of two minutes younger than me and the youngest of my mom's four children.

You know how people talk about middle child syndrome? Kara definitely had "the baby syndrome." Not in a bad way (all the time, LOL). She was the most spoiled, but she brings spunk, life, and laughter to our family. Her "just do it" mentality is the very reason she can write this book. *Bigger than Me* is truly her life's testimony. Every obstacle I can remember facing with her or seeing her go through always seems to bring her to the crossroads of a bigger purpose.

When she read excerpts of the book to me while she was writing, we both were overcome with emotion, some bad and some good. I started to reminisce about the day she revealed to me that she was going to live this lifestyle of being gay. We were in high school. This was over twenty years ago, and I still remember forming into a personal bodyguard and protector just in case anyone had something to say. Because this was my sister, she was different than friends around me and different than the people you gossiped or heard about in school who were gay. Then I could vividly see the moments she vowed to be done with this lifestyle.

"Note to self," I would say, "get up early tomorrow so you can be on time in case she needs you." We would talk on my way to work or on my way to just come and give her a hug so she could get through the day. Those days I will never forget. I remember telling her, "You are grieving, you are losing a whole life in all this. Go through the process, and let God hear you and heal you." I wanted so very badly to just take away the anguish I would see on her face, but I knew that was not my purpose in this. My purpose was to support her like the two-minute older sister that I am, LOL! I watched God allow her to be stripped, and then I watched Him save her and strengthen her. I have had a front-row seat in seeing her faith grow stronger and stronger. Her love for God is incredible. She truly believes His word and everything He has promised her.

Even though Kara and I had several years of physical separation due to her going off to college and me getting married and having children, we have always maintained our relationship. We still make it a point to call or text each other at 12:00 a.m. to say "Happy Birthday" (even when we are only rooms apart, LOL). I love, love my sister, y'all. I'm so grateful and honored to be asked to write this foreword. Kara isn't just my sister but my friend, one of my BFFE (best friends forever ever). Her story and life have inspired change in my life. She teaches me every day, with her actions, to do things afraid, take the risk, "what's the worst that can happen?" I pray this book will not only inspire but will bring vitality to the next chapter of your life.

—Kelli L. Fairbanks

INTROduction

"Will you marry me?"

She turned around while we were in the bathtub together, candles lit, music playing, ring in hand, and it was her birthday. "Yes!" she said.

We kissed and embraced each other as we were overjoyed about our future. But did we really have a future? At the time, same-sex marriage was not legal in our state, and never was same-sex marriage God's design, so what future did we really have? It's one thing to love someone with all your heart and they give you a reason to leave them, but it's another thing to love someone with all your heart and have "no reason" to leave them, other than God does not approve. But why? Why was my homosexual love wrong and heterosexual love right? What did God have against the LGBQIA+ community? The only way to get the answer to that question was to build a relationship with God.

My relationship with God would be like any other relationship; we talked and spent time together, but He was different from everyone else. He never lied to me, He never disappointed me, He loved me unconditionally, He never gave up on me, He was and still is always there for me, and because of that, I began to love Him more than the things He did not agree with. In my book, you will discover how God truly sees the LGBQIA+ community. You will learn what God did for me, He is the same God today, yesterday, and forevermore, and He will do the same thing for you.

BIGGER than ME is not just the title of my book; it's what God placed me on this earth for. To share my story with the world, to humble myself and allow my life to become my ministry. "I brought glory to you here on earth by completing the work you gave me to do" (John 17:4).

ROOT Cover-Up

I have to tell somebody. I can't keep this inside too much longer. I'm sure they already know. Why can't they just ask me and then I will tell them? I'll just wait until I'm eighteen, then nobody will be able to judge me. Thought after thought ran through my head as I went through middle and high school years dating, lusting, and loving girls. What made you start liking girls was a question I got so often, and the answer to that question was always, "I don't know. I just do." My response could have been a combination of, "Why is that any of your business?" or "Leave me alone if you're going to judge me," but I genuinely do not recall knowing why I had this attraction to girls the way I did.

I dated a few boys in middle school and high school, but I feel that was out of peer pressure and just thinking I had to because everyone else was doing it. I never felt as attracted to guys as I did girls, but as people say, maybe it was just a "phase" I was going through. The only phase I felt myself going through was liking girls more and more. I remember my first encounter with my same-sex attraction. It was my freshman year in high school, and I had asked my mom to stay at a teammate's house overnight. I distinctly remember having my Bible that night I went over because we were going to have Bible study while I was there. I'm not sure what scriptures we read and talked about, but soon after we were done, we went to bed. As I was sleeping, I felt my teammate put her arm around me, which was very new for me. Nobody in my family has ever held me like that; what was happening? I remember feeling awkward, but a good type of awkward, if that makes any sense, and uncomfortable, but I figured I would just last through the night, and I would not have to sleep over again if I did not want to. The next day, we went to school and I never mentioned it again. "The mind that opens up to a new idea never returns to its original size" (Albert Einstein). There was something in me that wanted to feel that "awkward" feeling again. I wanted to know what it was all about. I was "curious," and after that, my life would seem to not be the same.

After time to think about what happened and plan how I would dive into my curiosity, I had a friend come over to my house to hang out. It was late, and my mom and sister were not home this particular night. I would see her often because we went to the same church, and both our fire for Christ at the time caused us to just click with each other. I remember feeling awkward inside when I saw her at church and spoke with her on the phone, so I figured this is the perfect person. If she felt awkward about me, I was not sure, but I was going to find out. We were lying down on the bed talking, and I felt the feeling coming on even stronger. I remember putting my arm around her like my teammate did to me, and it seemed as if she received it. That made the feelings even stronger, so I began to touch her in other places. She never stopped me, but something in me stopped. The car ride to drop her off and come back was complete silence. The next day, she explained that she was not fond of what happened, and it never happened again. Of course, I was embarrassed. I did not know what to do or how to feel. Because of my church upbringing, I knew it was "wrong" anyway, so I tried to turn my attention to something else.

I began talking to a guy from the church who seemed to be interested in me. He would say nice things, hold my hand, and put his arm around me just like I had tried with my friend from church and like my teammate did to me. The awkward feeling was somewhat similar, so I went along with talking to him and eventually dating him. I don't remember thinking about girls during the time he and I were dating, so maybe it was just a phase. Unfortunately my junior year in high school, I discovered that he was seeing someone else, and that hurt me. That also triggered something in me to give up on men altogether. Because what good has any man done for me or to me anyway? It also triggered the question of what this awkward feeling was anyway. Is it lust? Is it love? Is it something that I even want or need? What was it? I mean it felt good, but it had also made me uncomfortable, embarrassed, and hurt. I was starting to think the awkward feeling was just a phase. I mean the only person that I felt that feeling from was my teammate, and she was, well, a **she**.

Was this the answer to my question? Was this the reason that I liked girls because I was introduced to the feeling of love/lust by my teammate? I looked up the definition for **root**, and these are some key parts that stood out to me: typically **underground**; the basic **cause**, **source**, or **origin** of something via numerous **branches**; established **deeply** and **firmly** (Oxford Languages).

I never told you that Dad was barely around. I remember sometimes going to where he lived to spend the night and a daddy-daughter basketball tournament we participated in. I remember going to get military ID cards with my dad, sisters, and brother and going to his wedding when he remarried. What I most remember though is when I learned in high school that he had adopted two other children. I remember how hurt I was to think that he would be a part of some other children's sports games, graduations, and proms but not mine. How angry I was that he chose to take care of other children before he would even take care of his own children. What did we do wrong? What did I do wrong? I don't remember ever feeling loved by dad though, like, "He's your dad, of course he loves you," is so cliché to me. Love is an action word, and those actions weren't love to me.

I failed to mention that mom struggled with her own issues of being a single mother of two sets of twins in addition to her mother passing at the age of fifteen. Needless to say, she was not taught how to be loved by my dad or how to love her children from her mom. I did not know that at the time, so it hurt to get yelled at for something I didn't do. It hurt to see her looking to other people for love and forgetting that we/I needed love too. She was not very affectionate toward us either, so hugs and "I love yous" were rarely given out or heard around the house.

I failed to mention that a family member made me have oral sex with him at a very young age often and introduced me to pornography. I was not aware of what was happening at the time, but I remember times when I thought I did not want to do it, but not because I knew it was wrong. We only watched pornography when he wanted to watch it, and that led to oral sex. I also never told you that I rode to Food Lion with a friend of the family and was penetrated with his fingers, kissed on, trapped in the truck, and told not to say a word when we got back to the house. I was going to a Christian private school at the time, and it was one particular person I felt I could trust to tell what had happened to me. After I told and specifically asked her not to tell, she did the right thing and told anyway. Being questioned by the investigator as if I was the one lying about what happened was draining and discouraging. I can't recall what ever happened to him. I think they gave him some type of probation or something, but at least I told, right? No damage was done, or was there?

> **One of our emotional needs is to feel loved. Therefore, in the same way you will do what it takes to survive physically, you will do what it takes to survive emotionally.**

One of our emotional needs is to feel loved. Therefore, in the same way you will do what it takes to survive physically, you will do what it takes to survive emotionally. Why? Because love is supposed to give us nourishment, love is what God commands from each and every one of us in Mark 12:31: "The second is equally important: Love your neighbor as yourself, no other commandment is greater than these." How does any of those situations that happened fulfill my need to be loved? That root of not being loved was getting deeper and deeper, and I had nothing that gave me nourishment to emotionally survive. My dad made me feel rejected, unwanted, and unloved. My mom never really showed affection toward us/me, and being molested by a male friend of the family and a male family member made me look at males a lot differently because they took advantage of me. None of those situations expressed love to me. "Storms make trees take deeper roots" (unknown), and since I am the tree and those are my storms, ask me your question again: what made me start liking girls?

Surely other people have gone through these very situations and turned out liking the opposite sex (my sister) was just a **cover-up**. Was I just using those experiences to make an excuse for what is considered wrong in so many people's eyes? Could a man, male, or boy even make me feel loved? Could my mom ever show me affection? It has to be possible. Relationships have been around since forever, and I have seen for myself healthy female and male relationships. Moms show their children affection all the time; I've seen it before on TV and at church. Maybe I'm just **different**. Maybe I am overexaggerating. It's a part of life. I'll get through this, just like everyone has, or will I?

Being raised in the church whether you want to be there or not, you hear things that may not make sense right then, but eventually a light bulb comes on. I've always heard this particular scripture but never took attention to it: "For I was born a sinner—yes, from the moment my mother conceived me" (Psalm 51:1 NLT). What! **we were all BORN SINNERS**? So was this God's plan all along? The Bible never says which sin; it just says **sin**. Contrary to what you might believe sin is sin, there is no big sin and small sin; there is no one sin that God accepts more than another sin.

We hear the LGBQIA+ community say sometimes that they were born this way, and although I do not agree with their motive behind saying that, as if it were a genetic thing, I cannot skip over the fact that the **root** of liking girls has been **covered up** because I was born into sin even though it was one that I chose to nourish. We know that God did not make "Adam and Steve," but he made Adam and Eve, and because of their downfall, they created the sin that we all are born into, but in the words of Kayne West, "What if Eve made apple juice? You gon' do what Adam do? Or say, 'Baby let's put this back on the tree…'" The choice is ours.

It was important for me to begin my story with what I believe are the roots of my homosexual lifestyle choice, not to make an excuse or blame anyone, but so that you understand I do not regret who I was. I do not condemn myself or anyone else who has been or is a part of the LGBQIA+ community. We all have underground causes and roots as to why we make certain lifestyle choices, which makes for a great book. I am so far from perfect while even writing this book, but I understand that it is part of my purpose in life to face my truths and share my journey because it's **BIGGER than ME**. My pastor says, in order to be delivered from any situation, you must "face it, trace it, and then you can erase it" (Apostle Johnny L. Magee Jr.). My heart while you continue to read is for you to be able to face your truths, trace your roots, and together we both can continue to be delivered and get closer to God. He that the Son has set free is free indeed (John 8:36)! To God be the glory!

LIfeSTYLE

Now where was I? Oh yeah, the boy was seeing someone else, and it hurt my feelings, so that was that…moving right along. I believe this is where I began to learn who I thought I was at the time. My emotional survivor mode took over, and I went crawling right back to my teammate. Now when I say crawling back, I don't mean I went asking to be her girlfriend or anything; I just started to find ways to be around her more, whether in school or outside of school.

My sister and I had our own set of friends mainly because I played sports and she didn't, so we didn't really hang out much in school or outside of school because I would usually stay back for basketball practice or be at my teammate's house. The more I hung out with my teammate, I began to pick up on the way she acted and dressed. Her pants and shirt were big, a little saggy, and her voice was deeper than most girls, that I knew anyway. I also started to notice other people on the team who acted and dressed like her too. Outside looking in, they were having fun all the time, a lot of people knew of them, and they felt loved—exactly what high school was supposed to be like, right? This could be the last time you ever hear me say this; I wanted to be like them, but how? My godmother was buying a lot of my clothes, and the ones my mom gave me money to buy fit tight and came from the girls' section. My voice was not even close to deep, and everybody knew I went to church, so why would they think I liked girls? It was at that moment we got a new teammate. She was from a different state, she was attractive, and she was not shy at all. Most importantly, she did not know anything about me, so this might just work. I was a cool person if, I had to say so myself, easy to get along with and outgoing. It seemed that people enjoyed my company, and I was not shy either.

As captain of the team, I got to show her around the school and the neighborhood. We both played the same position, so for me, it was war in practice, but all love/lust/like after practice. I walked her home some days after practice and even spent the night a few times. This was actually happening. I was getting that awkward feeling back, and it felt so good. I don't remember distinctly if I made the first move or if she did, but since it's my book, she kissed me first. It was not something we had ever talked about, so it's safe to say she was feeling the love/lust/like feeling too. I was happy just thinking in my head that she was my girlfriend. I didn't have to change the way I dressed; nobody thought any differently of me, that I knew of anyway, and I was finally like the rest of my teammates.

A few months passed, and since I said earlier that she kissed me first (seriously, don't quote me on that), I'll take the responsibility of asking her to be my girlfriend. To my surprise, she said yes, and I officially had my first girlfriend. Now that I have a girlfriend, I have to change the way I talk, dress, and act, right? I was still in the closet (hiding my sexuality), so if I changed the way I dressed or acted, people would be sure to notice and begin to label me. Little did I know, people were already labeling me because everyone but me could see that I was changing. I didn't talk in church the same; I was hanging around my teammates more and more; my new best friend looked, dressed, and carried herself like a boy; and I'm sure I was super protective over my new girlfriend because I didn't want her or that feeling to go away.

I began to hear the little birdies talking about me, calling me gay, and claiming all of these girls I was talking to. Girls would start to flock to me, partly because of who I was hanging around, and the other part is because as soon as you start dating someone, here comes the world trying to date you as if they didn't know when you were single. We talked for a few months longer, but then she decided that she did not want to be with me anymore. It was beginning to be too much pressure for her because she did not want people to know about her either. Her guardians were beginning to ask questions of her, and because she was the "new kid on the block" and played every sport at the school, the boys were fond of her as well. I do not recall being hurt per se because I felt like I had been here before in regard to the feeling of rejection. I knew I would still see her, and we could remain friends too, so that may have comforted me as well.

So what's next? Do I look for another girlfriend, or do I just go back to the old, unhappy me? You guessed correctly; let the search begin! There was no way at that time I was going back to being "unhappy." This new lifestyle was just being established, and the feeling was worth giving it another try.

My best friend was working at a fast-food restaurant, so I figured I would get a job to keep me occupied and maybe meet people outside of school. Getting a job also meant having my own money and being able to buy my own clothes. Every paycheck, there was something to be bought: men's sneakers and then an outfit from the men's section to go with the sneakers. My clothes were bought big because that's how my teammates and best friend were wearing their clothes. I still had most of my girl clothes, though, because I still had to go to church and whatever church functions. But at school and work, you better believe I had on my "boy" clothes. I wanted to show that I was gay so that the girls would approach me, but I didn't want to actually come out of my mouth and say I was gay because I would have to face being judged by my family members who didn't approve of a gay lifestyle, especially the people at church. It was a daily battle sneaking around the house so my mom and sister would not find out, lying to the boys at school when they asked if I was gay, defending myself on the team because some of my teammates did not like girls, and they gossiped to the rest of the school that I did. I dropped out of almost everything I was a part of at the church because of basketball and my job, is what I told them, but really because I felt so condemned. Nonetheless, the feeling I was searching for was worthy of the challenge.

Okay, so I got the money, I got the clothes, I've had my first girlfriend, and I'm partially okay with who I am becoming. Church is mainly out of the way, so let's get to it. My teammates were like female jocks. They went after the cheerleaders because they played a sport, like how every football player is in the movies. There was one particular cheerleader that I liked; she looked similar to my first girlfriend, which could be where the attraction came from, but I knew she was not into girls. I'm not sure where this idea came from that everybody likes me, and if I can just have a funny conversation with her, she will eventually like me too, but that was my plan. We were in the same graduating class, and I think I had a Spanish class with her. They practiced when we practiced, so I had my opportunities. I was cool with some of the other cheerleaders on the team already, and one lucky day, I was invited to a little kick back they were having **at her house**! Come on now, is this really happening again? Is God answering my prayers? I mean, I was still going to church. (Just so you know, the answer to any prayer that is not in God's will is a big fat **no**. I was lusting after women, which is the devil's line of work, and he continued to put situations in front of me because he knew I would bite [1 Corinthians 7:5; 2 Corinthians 11:14].). One of the other cheerleaders rode with me, but as I pulled up to her house, I was still nervous as I didn't know what. I had a pep talk with myself that went something like this: *Just be cool, don't sit too close. If she scoots over to you, then you know what time it is. If she doesn't, then try to say something that might make her, but if she likes you, she likes you, and if she doesn't, then she doesn't.*

> **Just so you know, the answer to any prayer that is not in God's will is a big fat no.**

She greeted us at the door, and we just sat upstairs in one of the four rooms they had and talked about everything that was going on at school. The topic of being gay came up, and I didn't say too much, but I did mention that I didn't see anything wrong with it. Her response was that she didn't care if people were; she just was not like that. I tried to hit her with a "don't knock it until you try it" quote, but that didn't work, LOL. At least I got invited over, right? Trust me, that gave me some points with my teammates and made some of the guys a little jealous too, so I was well on my way to getting the hang of this gay lifestyle.

My senior year in high school, it would get real. I really started to pull away from church, especially because my mom was not home often, and my sister and I had a choice to not go. My wardrobe was filled up with boy clothes and shoes, and we were winning in basketball, so that took things to a whole different level.

My eyes were beginning to open to so many other players from different teams who were gay, including some of their cheerleaders. The team would talk about some of the teachers at the school who "could get it," but I was not that brave at all, to approach them is what I mean, because there were two teachers that I had a serious crush on. By now, most people at school knew I liked and dated girls by my actions because I had yet to actually come out and say that I was. I was old enough to get into the clubs now, and if I wasn't, I got in! My first club experience was with my best friend in the fabulous city of Norfolk, Virginia.

I put on the best outfit I could put together, put my hair in a ponytail (which at that time, most gay girls who took on the male role would get their hair **cornrowed**, but I was not at that stage yet), had enough money to get in the club, and then lied to my mom about where I was going. It was on! When we got to the club, I could not believe my eyes. It was an entire community of gay people like I had never seen before. I had known that there were boys who were gay too, but this was beyond me. I saw girls dress like boys, but to not be able to tell if I was looking at a girl or a boy was somewhat scary for me.

The church inside of me immediately said **Sodom and Gomorrah**! So if you are familiar with the story of Sodom and Gomorrah, you know exactly what I'm saying. But if you are not, let me explain. You know the saying, "What happens in Vegas stays in Vegas"? Well, yeah, that's Sodom and Gomorrah. The city where anything went, from sexual immorality to alcohol and drugs, the city that God destroyed, and when I say destroyed, I am saying not one person was left alive in that city when He was finished with them. They had gotten so far from God by doing all kinds of sinful things that they were not thinking anything about God. So fear gripped my heart immediately; this was not who I was. I just wanted to feel loved; I didn't want to die doing it.

We stayed in the club for a few hours, and I tried my best to enjoy myself. After we left, we went to IHOP. Our waitress was a high school student, tall, light-skinned, and very pretty. I remember getting our drinks, and she forgot to bring me a straw. When she got back, I joked around with her about keeping the straws for herself and then found out what high school she went to and that she used to play basketball. I'm not sure what else I said, but before we left, she snuck her phone number onto the wrapper from the straw, and that made my whole night.

Do you know what this means? I have something about me that says I am gay without even saying "I'm gay," and anybody else who is gay will be able to detect it without having to say they are gay either, aka **gaydar**. I was officially official. In biblical terms, Christ was no longer my father; the devil was, and I would now begin to do things of the devil (John 8:44).

I called her, not right away because I wanted to play hard to get, but the thought of somebody asking me out did something to my ego. She sounded even better on the phone; her voice did something to my soul. It didn't take long for us to establish that we were girlfriends because back then, more than now anyway, Gay 101 says you're my girlfriend after a few days of talking on the phone all night.

She had a car, so she would come and get me from work sometimes. My mom still was not home much, so I would invite her over some days, and we would chill. Everything was going smoothly until my best friend told me about another girl who liked me who went to Booker T. High School.

Let's start with how bad, a good bad, everyone thought the cheerleaders at Booker T. were at that time. Let me also mention that the girl who liked me was talking to a player on the team at Booker T. who was better than me and older than me. Let me also mention that Booker T. was our rivals, and to date somebody from there would not make them happy.

Two girls liking me at the same time? This was the first time I had ever been in this situation. What was a girl supposed to do? I fought it for as long as I could, but the devil knew my pattern, and he made sure I didn't feel loved one time by my girlfriend, and it pushed me to give out my number to the other girl.

The thing about the devil is that he always sets you up for failure. He will bedazzle that thing and make that grass look so much greener, and once you fall for it, he takes the green screen off, and now you are in this entire mess. Needless to say, I got caught up, and it was my first time hurting someone in that way and the first time I felt hurt in that way.

I was sad for days; my mom ended up being in DC for that weekend and needed me to come and pick her up. I had my CD player with me, listening to Jesse Powell's "If I" on repeat. After I tried to get her back several times and it didn't work, I just decided to chill out with having a girlfriend. One of my cheerleader friends from the school was digging me, so we would do our thing every now and then, so I was not missing a whole lot.

After my experience at the club, I was introduced to **weed and alcohol**. I was not a huge fan at first because my best friend started me off with a Long Island iced tea mix, and I didn't know how to actually inhale the smoke, so it had no effect on me whatsoever. I needed to take my lifestyle up another level since I didn't have a girlfriend at the time, and I needed something to take away that disappointed feeling. So when I went to my brother's house, I learned how to smoke, and, man, did that take all my cares away. Or did it? It's funny how we use everything but God to get over our hurts and disappointments. I knew better because after all the other times I was hurt, the church helped me to feel better, but I had left the church, and the church (the God that was inside of me) had left me. I was so busy trying to **fix my own life** that I didn't realize I needed a plan, which I didn't have anyway. But God knows the plans for our lives, plans that are for good and not for evil, plans that give us a hopeful future (Jeremiah 29:11).

My mom started to be home more, and because I was comfortable with the way I was, I could not hide it too much. I tried to stay at my brother's house during the times I was not at work because he stayed up the street, or I had my best friend come over, or I would say I was going over there, but that only worked for so long. I could tell my mom was starting to get suspicious, but I had no plan as to how I was going to tell her. I had a few months before graduation and my eighteenth birthday, so if I could just hold off until then, I would be good.

Well, club experience number 2 would lead to me staying out until two in the morning with my best friend. She could not go home because her guardian was not having it. I was well past the time for me to be in the house because, as I told you, my mom was getting suspicious, so she gave me a curfew that night. We just went to my brother's house and spent the night. The next morning, we both went home because we got word that my best friend's guardian was calling the police, and we didn't want any part of that.

My mom was in her prayer room / office, she called me in the room, and I could see the hurt and disappointment on her face. With a very low voice, she asked, "What is going on?"

I tried to fight the question at first. "Nothing, I don't understand why I had a curfew. We were right at my brother's house."

She said a few things to that, but we both knew what she was really asking, so she asked again, "What's going on with you?"

I took a deep breath and said to myself, *Here goes everything…* **"I'm gay."**

WHERE DID all my GIRLFRIENDS GO?

Dead silence went through the room. It was out; I finally said what I didn't want to say. I finally told my mom what I didn't want to tell her because I thought the love she did show was going to be gone. I also knew that once I actually admitted to being gay, I had actually received my lifestyle, and there was no turning back. It was more sweet than bitter because I, at least, felt a little weight off my shoulders because I didn't have to hide anymore. I waited for her to say something, but I got nothing.

Next thing I remember, I was sitting in her lap, and we were both crying. My mom was crushed; I could feel and see the disappointment all over her face and her body language. It was as if the same thing that I did not want to happen with losing her love happened to her because she felt as if she lost me. For the next three days, my mom did not utter one word to me. Can you imagine how that felt? I imagine it's how Jesus felt when he was on the cross, and he was crying out to His father, "My God, My God, why hast thou forsaken me?" (Matthew 27:46). This was the moment when Jesus took on every last one of our sins, but God turned His back on Jesus because He was too holy to be in the presence of all that sin. He was asking His father a question. He didn't really believe that His father would never love or talk to Him again, but for that one moment, He understood the prophecy had to be fulfilled, yet He still spoke out of hurt because He was still human.

I knew I was going to tell her eventually, and I figured she would be mad versus hurt, but I never knew that she would just disown me for three whole days. Was I tainted with so much sin that she couldn't speak to me or be around me? Was she planning to kick me out, like I've heard so many other stories when people's parents find out their son or daughter is gay? Was being gay really this bad like at least I told her the truth? Why couldn't she see that I just wanted to be loved, not so much that I was gay? Why wasn't she happy for the fact that someone was showing me love and affection and it made me happy?

We didn't have this great relationship anyway, but she still was my mom. I didn't want to lose her like that. Rejection gripped my heart even more, but I wasn't new to this, so fine, be like that; you don't have to worry about me for long. Only a few months left until graduation and my birthday, and I would be eighteen and off to college shortly after that. I was not sure what college I would attend before that situation, but after her treating me like some kind of disease for those three days, I knew I needed to go away. My sister went to Norfolk State, which was right up the street, mainly because she was pregnant and had to work and go to school, but I needed a new scenery. I was afraid to go too far because I was the youngest, spoiled, and depended on a lot of people at home, but those people were scattering like roaches once I admitted to being gay, so I had to depend on myself now. I went to Chowan College, where I was recruited to play basketball. It was far enough away from home that it would feel as if I was gone, but could come back at any time of the day if I wanted.

After the three days were up, my mom tried to explain what she was feeling, but by then, it didn't matter to me. She said she was blindsided by my lifestyle. It made her feel like this horrible parent. She blamed herself for who I had become, and in the same breath, I felt like she gave me hell up until I left for college. I think she thought that if she could keep me in the house and keep my friends out of the house that the gay would go away.

My mom got so desperate one time, for lack of a better word, that she confronted my godmother from church because she thought that I was dating her. Now my godmother had already cut me off from buying me clothes and really even being in my life as much because she was not pleased when I told her about my decision to date girls either. I thought she was someone I could trust not to judge me. I thought she would love me anyway because our bond was pretty strong. I would spend the night with her and my godsister; she would pick me up for church, we would go out to eat, and things like that, more so too because my mom was not around, but all that began to fade away. It was right around Mother's Day because I had gotten my godmother and my mom a card, and they both had "mom" on them. My mom opened both of them, one of her ways to give me hell was that I had no privacy whatsoever and interpreted the card in a way that she thought my godmother and I were dating. After that, my godmother was out of the picture for the most part. She somewhat came back around in my college days only because she was always proud of my hard work in school and on the court, but in college, I went up a whole 'nother level when it came to dating girls, so she didn't come around too much.

Unfortunately, my mom and godmother weren't the only ones who turned their back on me. I had a few friends at the church that I would hang out with sometimes and spend the night at their houses. One particular girl was like a little sister to me. It was actually three of us. I was the middle friend; the oldest friend was the one discussed earlier whom I told I was molested by the family friend, and then my "little sister" was the youngest friend. She had a good relationship with her mom, and they talked about everything. I was never attracted to her in that way, but my biological sisters and I did not have a great relationship, and having those two at the time made me feel a family type of love.

Her mom got wind that I was gay, and she demanded that she not talk to me again. I was not allowed to go over to their house anymore, and she couldn't even speak to me if she saw me in church. She did not want any of my "gayness" to rub off on her daughter because being gay was contagious in some kind of way. The looks her mom gave me any time she saw me at church were a death stare from hell. Now how in the world could a deacon from the church make me feel like I had leprosy? Biblically leprosy was the one disease that not one person messed around with other than Jesus. **Leprosy** was an inward disease often started with secret sins, where only we will feel the tenderness. Then it begins to show itself in public ("5 Ways Leprosy Is a Picture of Sin," 2018). It was very contagious in the Bible, and it meant that you were cursed and a devil if you had it. Could this be true, like was being gay a modern-day form of leprosy? The more people that were disappearing from my life, the more it felt that way.

At least I still had my best friend from the church. Surely she wouldn't abandon me over wanting to feel loved, because that's really why I was gay. Females showed me love better than males did. My mom and dad's love was questionable and not the same feeling I got when I was with my girlfriends. My brother and sisters' love was a blur because we really didn't have that close of a relationship, my godmother's love seemed conditional, and the love of my "little sister's" mom was judgmental. Everyone else was being loved the way they needed and wanted to be; why couldn't I? My best friends' parents were like family too, really to everyone in the church. Her dad was called uncle, and her mom was called aunt. They were pretty popular in the church, and it was almost like if you associated with them, you were loved by everyone else in the church. We became friends because we both went to the school at the church, which she only stayed for a year, but we were also on the dance team at church, so we kept in contact with each other.

I remember writing her this letter expressing my feelings of gratitude for being my friend despite of what I told her about me being gay. I was appreciative of being able to talk to her about anything, and I asked her to be and told her that she was my best friend. She felt that I was her best friend too, and from there we were best friends. That wouldn't last long though because her mom got a little birdie in her ear that I was gay, and she did not want that to rub off on her daughter either. I will never forget the day my best friend, her mom, her dad, and myself went up to the little room in their home, and they explained that my lifestyle choice was not of God and that I was not allowed to come around anymore. It was her mom more than her dad, but they were married, so the whole "I gotta support my wife in front of you" thing happened.

I was devastated; why didn't she stick up for me? Why couldn't she just rebel against her parents this one time? I thought best friends were always best friends. Yet again I was getting rejected by someone whom I thought should be showing me love. All of these people were "church" folk. Is this what Jesus is like? Is this what He is teaching the people of the "church" to be like?

> **"The only difference between the saint and the sinner is that every saint has a past and every sinner has a future" (Oscar Wilde).**

I'm never going back to church; my mom won't be able to make me once I get into college anyway. I'll have any excuse not to go because I won't be home to attend church, but my real reason is that apparently God doesn't accept sinners, so what's the point of me going? That was so far from the truth. God is not even close to how my mom, godmother, and church friends' parents acted toward me. God is **love** (1 John 4:8)! It clearly says in the Bible that God came for the lost; he hung around the sinners. So why was everybody leaving me, disowning me, rejecting me, abandoning me just because I was gay? Like what kind of church people were they? The same gay person I was, the same way they labeled me, I labeled them. I gave them the title **church people**, which, to me, meant they were perfect like Jesus, they would do everything Jesus would do, they would love no matter what, they would treat me the same no matter what, and they would draw closer to me because of my sin, not push away because of it. Yet the reality of it was that they weren't church people; they were just people who went to church. They were human just like I was human. They were sinners just like I was a sinner. I was just a person who was gay. God had to deal with their ways just like he had to deal with my ways. We all were being displeasing to God, but they chose to see my sin differently than theirs. The Bible references that no one sin is bigger than the other: Romans 3:23, James 2:10, Matthew 7:3, Matthew 12:31. We all fall short of God's glorious standards, so whether you go to church or not, claim to be a Christian or not, you are still a sinner in God's eyes, and it's only by his grace that we see new mercy every day. If you go through life basing your decisions on other people's reactions, you are going to be miserable, and that is not God's plan for any of our lives. Yet if you go through life basing your decisions on God's reactions, you will have life and have it more abundantly. "The only difference between the saint and the sinner is that every saint has a past and every sinner has a future" (Oscar Wilde).

INSIDE her WORLD

I definitely was no saint, and the only future I saw myself having was being with girls because that's who I had become. I accepted the fact that this was God's plan for my life because He wanted me to be loved, and this was the only way I knew love. That's why He created Eve so that Adam would be loved by someone physically here with him in addition to God's love. The only difference between me and Adam was that he was a he, and I was a she. The problem with that was that it was not the way God intended for me to be loved. There is something in all of us called conviction, and it was something that I experienced every now and then when I was in college and even more after college.

I remember dating one girl on the basketball team, and we would go to her aunt's house sometimes on the weekend because that was the closest family she had at the time. That did not last long because her aunt was a Christian, and she figured out that we were in a relationship, so she did what everyone else did and threatened to cut her niece off if she did not stop talking to me in that way. So we had to end our relationship. I think this forced me to go back to church, and I remember getting baptized shortly after and doing my best to not like girls anymore.

To no surprise, going cold turkey when deciding not to be gay anymore is not quite the way it works. At the time, I did not understand that God was not asking for my sexuality more than he was asking for me to enter into a relationship with Him. It was too hard not to like girls because I was all around them, they made me feel good, and they were all I had while away at college. My teammate and I secretly began dating again, but then I was being reckless with some other girls, which opened up the door for a guy to sweep her off her feet, and we would not date ever again.

After that, I would go up another four levels. It seemed like in my lesbian lifestyle, because I would mess around with quite a few other girls in college and back at home, I was like Deuce Bigalow or somebody. Matthew 12:45 talks about this very thing when the demon (being gay) leaves you and tries to find someone else to enter but can't, so the demon "finds seven other spirits more evil than itself, and they all return to the person and live there. And so that person is worse off than before." That person would be me because God would not be a thought for another three years.

After college, I had to come back and live with my mom for a while, which was somewhat better because by this time, I was twenty-two years old, and it was like what could she really say about my lifestyle? She still was not pleased with it, I could just tell by her body language most days, and we did not have much conversation while I was home. So I did my best to not be home much because I did not want to deal with the negative energy. Maybe five months later, I met a girl I was really interested in, and remember when I said earlier in Gay 101 how quickly the LGBQIA+ community moves in with each other? Well, we were living together in no time.

Moving in with her would be one of my first **serious relationships**. It was labeled serious because I had adult responsibilities while living with her. Responsibilities such as paying rent and being a third parent to the kids she had. It would also be the first time that I would have to control any other feelings that I was having for anyone else. I couldn't just lock her out of my college dorm room hiding another girl in there. I was not able to go home on the weekend and entertain the girls that I was messing with on the side and then come back home to her as if nothing ever happened. I had to be faithful; I had to actually work to keep this relationship, or it was move back in with my mom, and that was not happening.

The great part about it was that I genuinely was feeling this girl, or should I say woman. She was a few years older than me, which in my mind made me feel like a female Casanova. She loved me so hard, and she spoiled me. Some kind of way, she knew my love language because she always seemed to say the right things (number 1 love language: words of affirmation). She kept my focus on her and only her. Just like a lot of relationships, we would have our ups and downs, but we continued to rock with each other.

Years before they were even considering same-sex marriage, I went as far as proposing to her, and she said yes. We had an engagement dinner and everything. I invited my family, but they were not in attendance. I can't remember exactly how long after the engagement, but I distinctly remember having a dream that went something like this. I was floating in the air for a while to eventually land at this place. When I got there, I walked through this huge room that looked like a church. Inside the room were pews, and on those pews, I noticed my mom and my two sisters sitting there, crying. I walked over to ask them what was wrong, but no one answered me. I walked away crying and found myself in another room. I was on my knees crying and begging God to give me another chance when I looked up, standing in the doorway was a man looking at me. The look he gave me was like the famous death stare your parents give you when they were about to beat you in 2.5 seconds if you didn't do what they had asked you to do. After the look, he just walked away. I remember waking up, and my breathing was as if I was underwater longer than I should have been. **I was shook**! Immediately I thought the dream was a vision of my sisters and my mom in a room where everyone was going to heaven, and I was in the room alone because I was going to hell. I thought the man standing in the doorway was God, and He was looking at me as if I had disappointed Him. The dream seemed so real; I had never experienced God in this way. Was it God? Why did this dream feel so real, what was happening?

After the dream, I did what most of y'all would have done: made sure I was in somebody's church that Sunday. Hell was not a place I wanted to be, so if God was going to be nice enough to come speak to me in my dream, I was going to be smart enough to at least go back to church. It's sad that it took a scare for me to acknowledge God, but I know now that God will soften or harden your heart in order to get your attention. I didn't tell my fiancée what was going on. I just suggested we go to church with her mom on Sunday. This would be my first time back in the church in years, but I was sure not a whole lot had changed, so I just prepared myself for the stares I would get because of the button-up shirt and khakis I was wearing and the attention we would get walking in as a couple with two kids. I honestly have no clue what the message was about, and not one time did I feel the presence of God in there. After church, I was trying to make a quick dash, but her mom wanted us to meet everybody and talk like most people do after church.

When we got home, the dream was still ringing in my spirit, but I just felt like Rome was not built in a day, so I just need to make sure I am in church next Sunday too. We would try some other churches, mainly the one my mom and sister went to, or we would go back to the church her mom went to, but my actions and heart were still the same. Eventually, we got into some kind of argument, and she mentioned she was not going back to church because we were still doing the same things, and I did what people do when they want to keep the peace in their home: I said okay. We would go through a bunch of other things after that moment, and it would eventually cause us to split up. This would not be the last time God would deal with me.

It seemed like every last week of December, I would feel this urge to just want to be different. Different like not wanting to be gay and please God. I remember crying to myself, hearing gospel songs, and just feeling so convicted with who I was for that entire week if not the week before too. I wanted to do right, but my flesh was weak and wanted to do the wrong thing, and my flesh won almost every time. Those seven demons would come back even stronger. My college roommate and I would eventually get a place together, but a few years later, I would get my own place. I was a teacher and coaching basketball, so it seemed as if I had my life together. Like I was that one friend that my other friends told their girlfriends they were with, especially when they weren't with me, because I was the one who had their "head on straight." I was the one who could be trusted. Let me be the first one to tell you moving by myself was the worst thing that happened to me spiritually. Having my own apartment was like **bringing Vegas to me**. Whatever happened at my house had better stay at my house. Cookouts, parties, rendezvous, ménage à trois (threesomes), drugs, alcohol, sleepovers, girls, girls, and more girls. I had moved Satan right in and kicked God right out. What I didn't realize is that God was still dealing with me. My heart was being hardened as I was **ignoring God**. I would soon find myself being evicted from my apartment, mainly because I did not have it all together, and I was not being a good steward of my finances. God could not bless me financially because He did not trust me with the finances He was providing for me in the first place. I moved in with my best friend from high school for a few months, and then I would find myself in another serious relationship. My college best friend introduced me to a girl she worked with who was straight, but that did not mean much to me. She was a cool person to hang out with, especially because she smoked. Her accent and her strong attitude gave me something to pick with her about and carry a conversation. I did not have my own place, and I was not technically dating anyone, so I focused my attention on her. I found myself at her house often and then having conversations about living together.

Before we moved in with each other, she would go to church on Sunday with her aunt, and I would stay at the house until she got back. One day, I did go to church with her, and just like before, church people had not changed. I got looks from the church people and her aunt, and I don't remember what the preacher was talking about because I was really just there to be with her. The only other time I would go to church with her was when her aunt wrote a play, and we went to support and when her cousin got married.

During the time she and I were together, my sister and mom were attending a new church. I think my sister invited us because it was friends and family day, so we decided to go. From the first time I stepped foot in that church, I knew something was different. I didn't feel like people were staring at me; I didn't feel like I was in Judge City. I felt loved with all the hugs I got; I felt comfortable with being able to clap my hands and sing the songs that I knew. I felt like if I was going to continue to come to church, I would give this church another try. The message, if I'm not mistaken, was about angels. I don't think I had ever heard a preacher talk about angels, but it caught my attention, and I learned that angels were real and that I had my own personal guardian angel, which didn't surprise me because that can only explain all the mess I got myself into but someone or something else had gotten me out of. Could this church be what I needed to keep coming to church and getting to know Christ better? We went back to the church the following Sunday and the Sunday after that and the Sunday after. I even found myself going to Bible study on Wednesday.

We ended up moving to Virginia Beach because she was living in Portsmouth at the time, which made church even more convenient. I did not want to give up my relationship with her because I liked her a lot, I felt she needed me because of discussions we had had before, and I told her I was going to treat her right and be there for her, but I at least felt better knowing I was not just ignoring God anymore. I dreaded the day the pastor would talk about homosexuality because I was learning so much, and I believed and trusted every word that came from his mouth. I couldn't not believe what he would say about homosexuality but believed everything else he was saying.

> **I would invite my friends to church, and I would begin to speak up about God even though my lifestyle was still the same.**

Nonetheless, God would start to deal with me again; he would soften my heart this time to give my life back to Him in May of 2014. After that day, my life would **change**. As I was coming from the back of the church where they talk to you a little about salvation and get your information to keep in contact with you, one of the elders was standing at the door, and the next words that would come out of his mouth sounded like God was literally speaking through him. He looked me dead in my eyes and said, "Your life will never be the same again." I felt those words, I didn't know what they actually meant at the time or how he even knew what my life was like, but I knew my life was not going to be the same. I would find myself feeling convicted more times than not. I would go on no drinking and smoking binges because I was feeling bad for committing **all the sins**, knowing I had just given my life to Christ. I would invite my friends to church, and I would begin to speak up about God even though my lifestyle was still the same.

My new relationship with God was just like a new relationship with that person you were dating; those first six months or two months in Christian life were golden. The way everything was going just right, everything was so blessed and highly favored, the way nothing could go wrong, it seemed that everything was working out for my good. The way you can't stop talking about the person, I couldn't stop talking about God, but my lifestyle was still the same.

God would visit me in another dream again after I had taken a turn for the worst and used drinking as my "savior." I was depressed because somewhere down the line, that perfect relationship takes a bad turn and then nothing seems to be what it was, and nothing is going right anymore. Where did God go? How did I get to becoming an alcoholic? Was God punishing me for not giving up my gay lifestyle? I was at church whenever I could be, I was telling people about Him, and I was even giving tithes and offerings. How wasn't that enough? The dream was just as clear as the first one and very similar. I would be floating again and find myself back in this building. The pews were still there, and my mom and sisters were still there, but this time they were not crying. I found myself back in the room alone crying. I looked up, and there He was again standing in the doorway. This time it was not a look of disappointment, but he spoke this time to tell me that I had to give it to Him. He never said what "it" was, but when he said it, it made me feel like this was strike 2. I woke up again as if I had stayed underwater too long and began to cry. I was not ready to give up being gay if that's what the "it" was.

This time my girlfriend was very aware of me crying, and she asked what was wrong. I told her that God was dealing with me and what I thought the "it" was that God required from me. Our relationship was not the best during that time anyway, so it seemed to be a little easier for me to trust God with the "it," or at least I thought. Time went by, and I made a decision to switch up some things in our relationship such as sleeping in the same bed. We were living in a three-bedroom townhome, and one of the rooms was technically mine. My bed and clothes were already set up in there, so it was just a matter of sleeping in my own room. We would still attend church sometimes together, sometimes not together.

It was one particular Sunday, June 28, 2015, and I had a calmness about me before going to church that day. Not that any other Sunday I didn't, but I was aware of what was going on in the world, that same-sex marriage had just been legalized, and my pastor does a good job of listening to God and speaking truth about what is going on in our world, so it was possible that it would be the topic for today. Stereotypically when you hear pastors speak about same-sex relationships, they are bashing, condemning, and making that group of people feel like God does not accept them and they are going to hell, which was so far from the truth because the Bible tells us that there is **nothing** that can separate us from God's **love** (Romans 8:39). So I could have very easily not gone to church that day because I was only a month in from rededicating my life back to Christ, and I was still living with my girlfriend at the time, but that peace that I felt that Sunday provoked me to go to church anyway.

The worship that morning was so filling, and I was ready to receive whatever was coming across the pulpit. Offering was over, and it was time for the word. My ears were all the way open to hear every word the pastor would say as he announced the title of the message, which was, "The Supreme Court has ruled, and God has not changed His mind." Now my heart would usually do flips when he prayed before teaching because for whatever reason, what I know now was the conviction in me, when he prayed that he "would not say anything perverted or contrary to that which is **sound** doctrine," I immediately thought he was coming for me. But my heart was still at the title; I was not fearful, I did not feel convicted, and I was at peace because I was in a place where I was ready to **RECEIVE the truth** about what I was dealing with.

He started by congratulating the LGBQIA+ community for receiving our civil rights. Wait, what? Did Pastor just say congratulations to the LGBQIA+ community? Yes and no. He was saying that everyone, regardless of who or what you are doing, we all should have civil rights, and he was congratulating the LGBQIA+ community for that. He was not congratulating the LGBQIA+ community for our sins.

it was not God's intended protocol, intended purpose, or His intended pleasure (Dr. Johnny L. Magee Jr.)

After giving scripture on where his title came from, he went on to explain why he believed, based on the scripture, that God is not for same-sex marriages. He gave three reasons why God isn't for same-sex marriage: it was not God's intended protocol, intended purpose, or His intended pleasure (Dr. Johnny L. Magee Jr.). His protocol or order was obvious, Adam and Eve, male and female. Notice how I wore male clothes, my teammates wanted their voices deep, we carried ourselves like males or in the LGBQIA+ community, we were considered "studs" (**stud** is defined as a young man thought to be very active sexually), and anybody who continued to dress feminine or ladylike was considered **fem** (short for feminine). We took on the male role because that is the order God intended in relationships.

The intended purpose of creating Eve was for her and Adam to be fruitful and multiply (Genesis 1:28). With same-sex relationships, this could not **biologically** take place. Even though I'm sure the LGBQIA+ community thinks they can argue this last point, as for God's intended pleasure, we have to understand that everything that feels good to us does not mean that it is good for us. A man's penis and a woman's vagina, once penetrated, literally connect their souls together and join them together as one, and that is the pleasure God intended in relationships, marriage specifically, when referring to God's intended pleasure. Woooooowwwwww! How can you argue that? How could I still say to myself, *This is just who I am*? That being with females was God's plan for my life? That was a lie from the enemy; it was a footpath that I had allowed the devil to keep me in.

The revelation of a footpath is that it's something **we** create by ourselves. It's like when you constantly walk in the grass to get to your front door because it's easier to walk through the yard and not around the yard. The more you continue to walk on the grass, it makes this pathway where the grass doesn't grow anymore, and so you just get used to walking in that path. The path was not supposed to be there, but you created it because you didn't want to take the **long way**. I learned the hard way that if you take shortcuts, you will get cut short. That was me, this whole time I looked for the easy way out. I wanted to do things my way, not God's way because that was taking too long. I needed instant gratification, I needed love right away, so I made my path, but it was not the path God had for me. This message would be the defining moment that would start this journey to give up who I created myself to be.

STRengTH

In Matthew 16:24, God tells His disciples that if they want to follow Him, they would have to give up their own way, take up their cross, and then follow Him. Salvation and deliverance are a process; it's something that has to be worked on every day. It's not one of those things where you say you're saved, and then there is no action behind it. It's one of those things where when you say it, you better mean it because there is so much work that comes with it, intentional work that does not just come naturally.

It was time to put my words of claiming to be saved and wanting to walk with God into action. It was time to take these dreams more seriously. It was time to not just be a hearer of the word but also a doer of the word. This was going to be one of the hardest things I've had to do in my life. It wasn't like admitting myself to AA classes and not drinking for nine months straight, which included turning down my friends and free drinks quite a bit.

After the first month I had been in the meetings, I took myself out because I was learning enough at church to know that death and life are in the power of the tongue. In every class, we would say that we were alcoholics, but we were actually trying to be free from alcohol, so I decided not to go back and be strong enough to not drink. I know that God helped me through those nine months, but seventeen years' worth of same-sex relationship, how was He going to get me through this one?

My friends were gay, and people I hung around with who weren't gay accepted the fact that I was. My conversation was the same. My actions toward other girls who didn't know of my dreams were the same. This was not looking good. In particular, there was one girl that I was on and off with for about **seven years**. My love for her was a lot different than the others, and everyone around me knew it. We have said things like, "It doesn't matter who is in our lives, we will always be there for each other," which really meant we could have each other whenever we wanted. If one person was going through it with their significant other at the time, the other person was right there to go through it with them, which really meant it was an opportunity to be with each other, so we took it.

There was definitely a soul tie there or a bond that was not ever thought to be broken. This time around, though, we both were saved, and we both were not in a relationship, so this was not the same, was it? She understood God, she was active in the church, and we could talk about Christ together. This had to be some bonus points for me in God's eye, right? We were still lusting and loving each other, but we were active in church. We talked about not sitting beside each other in church because I did not want to be "disrespect-ful" to God, but in the same breath, we said we were not going to get baptized because it was disrespectful to God for us to still be the way we were and get baptized. We used God's word to our advantage somewhat so that it would seem one way on the outside, but it was really a different way on the inside. We would continue to date and call ourselves working out the kinks that made us be on and off with each other for so long.

I was scared to ask her to be my girlfriend, a question I had never asked her before, because I felt in my heart the minute I asked her, God was going to begin to deal with me again. I asked anyway because I figured God was in our lives, so it was somewhat different.

Note: God being in our lives is not the same as God being the head of our lives. Technically, God is in everyone's life because He promised never to leave us or forsake us. However, Him being the head of your life means that what He says goes. It means that you are seeking Him first and foremost about any decisions you want to make. It means that you are going to be obedient to His word. It means you are choosing to think and live differently.

I don't even think it was a week after I asked her to be my girlfriend when God started to deal with me, SMH. I was scrolling on Instagram (IG) one day, and this quote stood out. I mean, immediately, I thought about myself when I read, "God cannot bless who you pretend to be." That hurt my feelings because I knew that was for me. I was still doing my best to be saved at church and at my job, but at home, I still had a girlfriend whom I loved more than God.

It was October 19, 2017, when I asked her to be my girlfriend. On December 5, 2017, she was out of town, and I was house-sitting. Remember when I said God normally deals with me at the end of December if not earlier? "Christmas had come early." God was dealing with me so heavily that night. I was so scared because I knew the time had come that I was really going to put my love for God to the test.

I remember calling her and trying to sound normal, but my voice kept crackling. She eventually asked the question I did not want to answer. "What's wrong?" It was like a fifteen-second pause from me and then a deep sigh. As I began to tell her that God was dealing with me about our relationship, the tears just started to flow. I honestly don't know how she heard a word I said because I couldn't stop crying, and then she was crying. I told her that God was dealing with me and that we were not going to be able to continue our relationship. I told her I didn't know what to do. I wanted to get baptized because I wanted to be serious with Christ, and I didn't feel that God was pleased with the fact that she was the only reason why I was not going to get baptized.

My actions toward her were different in those few months anyway because I was doing what I thought was my best to work on "not being gay." I wasn't saying "I love you" as much, I was not kissing or having sex with her as often, and I would not spend the night as much. I knew it was not going to happen in a day, but I could at least try. She noticed that I was being different and less intimate too, so it was not a huge surprise. She was more mad at God because we both believed we could be this power couple that was gay but still loved God and claimed being saved.

The very next day, I called her at least five times, and she did not answer. I was sick to my stomach. What was happening? Why didn't she want to talk to me? This is not my fault; we talked about this. We both agreed on doing our best to follow God better. I couldn't think straight; I did not sign up for these feelings I was having. I finally was around someone who I could use their phone to call her, so I did. To my surprise, she answered the phone.

I was so hurt I started to yell at her, "Why aren't **you** answering for me?" (I wanted to cry so bad, but I couldn't because I was around other people.) "I have called you five times today, anything could have been wrong."

Her response: "I just need some time to myself, I can't talk to you right now."

I don't know what I expected to happen after I called her that night to break up with her because of what God said, but it definitely was not this.

I sucked up how I felt until I got home that night and cried myself to sleep for the second night in a row. The Bible says that if we want to follow Christ, we must first deny ourselves and then take up our cross; this would be the start of my long walk to Calvary. I reached out to her every day after because I wanted us to get through this together. We just needed to take it one day at a time. I just needed her to be on the same page with me and do her best not to touch me the way she did, look at me the way she used to, or change her tone to normal when she spoke to me because I figured that would help me to turn from being gay.

Time would go by, and as long as I knew that she was not dealing with anybody else, I felt safer working on not being gay. Unfortunately, we would be dealing with this situation differently. While I was doing my best to follow God's way, I felt she was doing things her way. When I was feeling down and out, I would turn to God. I would pray, read a devotion, call her to try and talk, sit home by myself and cry it out, and I may have depended on alcohol here and there, which was not God's way, but I had my moments.

When she was feeling down and out, she would go out with a friend to get her mind off me. She was not calling me back some nights when she said she would, and although it hurt my feelings, I called myself trying to deal with it because this is what we had to do to keep our relationship as friends.

It was one particular night in February when God revealed to me that she was dealing with someone else. I was angry in my dream, hurt, crying, and I remember yelling at her. The next morning, I woke up to a phone call, which was her calling me back from last night, and her voice just sounded different. We talked for a minute or two, and then I asked what's up, what's wrong. She said nothing was wrong but there was something she needed to say. She said, "Remember when you asked me to tell you when I'm ready to start dating? Well, I'm ready to start dating."

I told her that I had just dreamed about it and I knew that she was going to tell me that. I asked her why she felt like she was ready to start dating, and her response was, "I don't know."

Now I didn't know this at the time, but God needed me to depend on Him to get me through this situation and not depend on knowing that she was not dating anyone else to get me through my deliverance.

> **"Strength doesn't come from what you can do; strength comes from overcoming the things you thought you couldn't" (unknown).**

"Strength doesn't come from what you can do; strength comes from overcoming the things you thought you couldn't" (unknown). This would be the next turning point in my walk to Calvary.

Thoughts flooded my mind when I got off the phone with her that morning. Who was he? It's only been two months; how in the world is she ready to date? How can she say she loves me but wants to be with someone else? I can't do this anymore, God. I don't want her to be with anyone else. It's not like I just broke up with her because I wanted to; I only broke up with her because walking with God required me to.

Every day was a struggle to either call and talk to her or not call and talk to her. If I called and she didn't answer, I would be angry and hurt. If I called and she did answer, I wanted to know why she didn't answer last time, and her response would make me angry and hurt again. We would argue about the way she was treating me, even though I knew it had to be different because she was not going to stay single forever. It was just too soon for me to deal with it coming from her so soon. Not to mention I felt so alone; I did not have anyone whom I believed I could talk to, to help me get through my brokenness. Yes, I still had friends, but their advice was, "This is just who you are. You are a good person. God is not going to be mad at you for loving her. You go to church, you obviously love God." Basically, it's okay to be with her, and I knew it wasn't.

March finally came, and it was time to be baptized. There was no turning back now. It had only been a month since she had been dating this guy, and my mind, heart, and body felt like it had been years. Being baptized meant showing everyone I invited and everyone who was there that I am going to be accountable for my actions from here on out. Both of us would get baptized on that day, so I thought it meant the same for her. In my eyes, my actions would get better and hers would get worse, and I would feel more depressed while she would feel happier.

I wondered how this was happening. I'm doing what you said, God, to the best of my ability, and this hurts like hell. How long would this walk to Calvary be? This cross is way too heavy for me. All the while, God was right there with me; I just was not allowing Him to help me.

In the month of April, I worked on not answering the phone every single time she called, and I got deeply into reading my Bible app because the devotions were helping me get through these tough times. Devotions about hurt, deliverance, changing the way I think, having peace, walking with Christ, and more. It worked more times than it didn't because we would have our moments when we would sleep with each other, which, of course, did not help anything. It only made me feel better at the moment because it confirmed that she was only with the guy because we couldn't be together and, at the same time, made me feel horrible knowing she would be with him the very next day.

Going into May, I was determined to do better, to be stronger. I was going to trust God more so that this knife in my heart could be taken out once and for all. If you know anything about God, then you know when you ask Him to help you trust Him more, He puts you in situations where you have to trust Him. And if you choose to trust Him or not, that's His way of helping. To be fair, God gave me so many dreams and visions of half the things that would eventually end up breaking me down and hurting me. I just didn't realize it until after it actually happened.

The first week of May, I met her at a family friend gathering, and everything was cool until I noticed a watch on her arm. When I questioned her about the watch, she literally laughed in my face and said it was her friend's. I asked why she had it on, and she said because he left it, and she was supposed to be meeting him later for him to get it. If you ever watched *Popeye* and the one part where he eats the spinach and he begins to get red and then steam comes from his head and pipe because he is about to snap, well, that was me without the spinach. This was test number 1.

I calmly told everyone that I was leaving, hugged her mom, sister, and her mom's friend, walked out of the house, got in my car, and pulled off. One of the devotions I was reading was called *Words to Live By*, and it was about taking the thoughts of the enemy and making them obedient to God's word. Every affirmation I could remember at the time, I quoted it, and it honestly calmed me down. I had already dreamed about them having sex with each other, but it hit differently when you know for a fact. I was crushed once again, and to add insult to injury, she called and asked why I left. I told her exactly how I felt, which included that if her family was not there, I would have punched her in her face for laughing in my face as if she didn't know that what she was going to say was going to stab my heart.

After that day, the dreams would become even more clear. I took a back seat for a little and continued to do all I could not to jump at her every waking call, but it would be hard. You see, she didn't want me to be with anybody either, and as long as she could keep me feeling like she loved me, she was okay with living a double life. I'm not calling her the enemy, but her actions were an example of how the enemy does us. He knows our patterns and what makes us go against God's plan, and he uses it against us just enough to keep us playing the fence of giving in to the flesh or surrendering to God. I couldn't do this by myself. I told God every day how much I loved her and wanted to be with her. I asked Him to take those feelings away, even though deep down, I didn't want Him to. I needed someone physical to be here with me to go through this with me.

I decided to reach out to my friends, but I specifically told them that I did not want to talk about her or what she and I were going through. That would at least help me not be in the house all day every day thinking about what she was doing.

First Lady's birthday would be approaching, and she was having a conference titled "Who Are You?" I told God and myself that I was expecting something from this conference because I was so tired of crying, and I was just drained. The conference would highlight these points: I am **valuable**, I am **acceptable**, I am **loveable**, I am **understandable**, and I am **exceptional**. The first letter of each word would spell out the word **value**, which is how God sees us. We are of **value** to Him.

All three days of the conference blessed my entire life. The first night was a concert by Shanna Wilson, and I remember shouting for the first time in **yeeeeeaarrrssss**. The next session would break down each of the words from God's point of view, and I could feel God just speaking to me the entire time. The last session would come from Dr. Renne Hornbuckle, and if you don't know her story, then you should go look her up. But her strength to get through her situation and her transparency about it all just freed me so much. It inspired me to go on IG and start a series I called "Bigger than Me." It was telling the world how God was dealing with me about my sexuality and what I was doing about it. People would reach out to me about feeling the same way and asking multiple questions because they wanted to be delivered too.

The walk to Calvary was starting to have some light at the end, but the enemy was not trying to let me have any parts of it. The next week was my birthday, and my sister and I would celebrate by having a movie-themed party. I invited all my friends, including her. I dressed up as Monica from *Love & Basketball,* and she was super turned on by it. We did not come to the party together, but we left together, and she stayed over for the rest of the day and the following day.

While she was there, we had a long conversation about our feelings, which included things we liked and didn't like, things we wanted to stop, and things that we were not going to stop. Now the aftermath was not as bad because I was accepting her way of dealing with things, and I was building this wall that said, "No matter what, I am valuable, acceptable, loveable, understandable, and exceptional," or at least I thought I was.

About a week or so later, I dreamed that he was over her house, and I woke up around two in the morning, hurt again and angry. I told her about my dream, and we talked about him not spending the night anymore. The same day, she said okay to him not staying anymore. I had another dream that night that he was there. I called her phone at two in the morning when I woke up, and she answered. I asked her the question I really did not want the answer to. Is he there? Her response was yes, but he was on the couch. I began to fuss because she had just told me that she wasn't going to let him stay anymore, and the same day he was there, and then I just got off the phone. This was test number 2; would I trust God to deal with the way I was feeling, or would I deal with my feelings on my own?

So this is the scene from the movies when the devil is on one shoulder, and God is on the other shoulder, but it was happening in real life. So I did what everybody in the movies does: I plucked God right off my shoulder and took in the advice of the devil. Next thing I knew, I was in my car going 70 mph on my way to her house. When I got there, the devil had been so kind to leave the garage door open for me, which meant I could walk right into her house, but God stepped in and suggested I call and say thanks for leaving the garage door open so that by the time I got out of the car, she was meeting me at the door that led to the house.

I literally felt like I was not myself. I felt stronger, I felt invincible, I felt enraged. You know how we say God works in mysterious ways? Well, it could have only been Him to make me consider in all my rage that if I did this, she might never talk to me again, which is not what I wanted, because that was the only thing that kept me from going in the house and making the biggest scene I could. I sat outside of her house for the rest of the night, crying, praying, trying to remember my affirmations. I had fallen asleep, and when I woke up, his car was still there. I cried more and got out of the car and walked to the park. I was so determined to talk to her; she needed to know how I felt like I loved her, I really did, but God was doing something in me that made me love Him more than her. Eventually, she came out to talk to me, and I couldn't stop crying. We ended up back at her house talking, and it made me feel somewhat better.

After a few hours, I went home, and she said she would call me later. When I got home, I beat myself up because I realized I had failed the test. I was 1 for 2, and God would not even wait for the next day when He gave me test number 3. She ended up taking too long to call me, so I began to text her. While texting, I just felt like she was lying to me, and so I was accusing her through the text and driving myself crazy at home. When she finally was able to talk, we argued again, but in that argument, God said something to her to say to me: "**You need to trust God**." I got off the phone with her and went into my bathroom, screamed at the top of my lungs, and cried out to God. I am trying to trust you, I am trusting you, this hurts, and He said to me so clearly with ALL your heart. That word **all** stood out so clear; I was only trusting God with the part of my heart that knew what she was and was not doing, I was only trusting God when I was having a good day, I was only trusting God when I felt like I was in control of my feelings, but that was not with **all** my heart. This is why Proverbs 3:5 is my favorite scripture in the Bible because it would change the direction of my life. The scripture reads, "Trust in the Lord with **all** your heart, and lean not on your **own** understanding."

From that moment on, every time I would feel like I couldn't handle it anymore, or I wanted to give up and turn back to my old ways, God would say **all** your heart, and I would repeat **all** my heart, and I would say to the situation or to the feeling, **all** means **you.** The rest of June and July would be rough because the only way to be healed was to go through rehab. The only way to really break through was to continue to be in situations where I had to trust God with all my heart.

July came, and I went to Kentucky and Chicago for about ten days on an AAU basketball assignment. I would continue Message Monday, and I would continue not talking to her every second, reading my devotions, and just doing my best to get stronger. When I got back, it seemed to be so important to her that she spent time with me because this was what we usually did when I went away or she went away for a while. I distinctly remember thinking she only wants my time so nobody else could have it, or at least she wanted to be the first one to see me since I had been gone for so long. I went with it and had brunch with her, then hung out with her and the kids for a while, but then that was that.

About two weeks later, it was her turn to leave for about seven days. I was still in my phase of not talking to her as much, even to the point where I fasted from talking to her the week she was leaving. I know that sounds strange that I fasted from talking to her, but fasting is simply giving up something that you feel you can't be without and replacing it with spending time with God and drawing closer to Him as He draws closer to you. Joel 2:12 says, "'Yet even now,' declares the Lord, 'return to me with all your heart with fasting.'" We did not talk often while she was there; however, when she came back, the expectation was that she would be pressed to see me the same way she was when I got back from my trip. Needless to say, that was not the case **at all!**

The part I want to get to is test number 4. So if you are keeping track, I am 1.5 for 3 because the last test I kind of trusted God, but I kind of didn't. Test number 4, she was on her way home, and the bus she was on broke down. I happened to text her to check on her, which was how I found that out, but then I didn't hear from her again until I checked on her that night, and she told me that she was home. We were supposed to link up when she got back, but she was tired and had some things to do, so she took a rain check for the next day. The next day she called, but the time she wanted to do anything was bad timing, so she said she would call me back later. I waited all day waiting for a callback. I told myself I would give her time to call me back because I did not want to be pressed about how long it was taking her to call me back.

Four o'clock, five o'clock, six o'clock, and still no call. Of course, my mind was everywhere, but I read my Bible and found some things to do around the house to keep me calm. Seven o'clock, eight o'clock, the phone rings. I let it ring a few times before answering, "What's up?"

Her: "Hey, what you doing?"

Immediately I knew something was up because of her tone.

Me: "Nothing, what have you been doing?"

She went on to explain what she had been doing all day, and then she mentioned that she was heading to Applebee's to get something to eat. My response was, "Oh, okay." Before we got off the phone this time, she made it her business to tell me that she was not going to be talking to me anymore that night. So basically, she was not calling me back.

After we get off the phone, my heart began to race, my thoughts began to take over me, and instead of going back to reading my Bible and finding things around the house to keep me calm, I began to think, and test number 4 was not looking good for me. I remembered that she told me one time where he lived, by accident, so I looked up the neighborhood. She just mentioned that she was going to Applebee's for dinner, so I found the closest Applebee's to the neighborhood, got in my car, and set in the parking lot as if I was on a real-life stakeout. I felt rage all over me, and nobody was going to tell me anything at that moment, not even God. Fifteen minutes later, they came walking out, he opened the door for her, got in the car, pulled off, and I was right behind them. I know this is deep, but God has delivered me from this situation, and I can laugh about this now. I watched way too many movies, like I was really trying not to be seen as I was following them, trying to keep my distance and everything. Unfortunately, I was not good at it, and I eventually lost them.

Plan B, call her until she picks up the phone. That did not work; onto plan C. Text her and let her know that I know where he lives and that she could either meet me somewhere to talk to me or I was coming there to talk to her. Third time's a charm because that worked. I immediately got a response. To make the story short, she met me at a 7-Eleven, and she said some very hurtful things to me, not so much mean things, but words that I would not expect from her, like I only have ten minutes of her time, and she had to go. Things like she's not leaving him to come and stay with me, and they haven't seen each other since before she left, so he wanted to see her, as if I didn't. Can you say **epic fail**? "It hurts the most when the person who made you feel special yesterday makes you feel so unwanted today" (unknown). If I had just trusted God to deal with the way I was feeling, none of this would be happening, but I didn't. I was 1.5 out of 4 chances, and God had given me to do what I asked Him to do for me in the first place, which was to help me trust Him.

We pulled off at the same time, and I followed her just a little, but then I gave up. I turned my phone off and went home. I was emotionally drained, and there was nothing else left to do. I kept my phone off for the next four days. I didn't want to keep looking to see if she was going to call; I did not want to be tempted to text or call her. I was too weak, too vulnerable. 1.5 out of 4 is a big fat F for the faint at heart.

I called her when I turned my phone back on four days later, and she had not picked up the phone one time to call or even text me. But that's what I wanted, right? "God causes all things to work together for the good of those who love Him" (Romans 8:28 NLT), and although I was failing the test, God was pushing me closer to Him.

Toward the end of that month, I joined the mime ministry at church. Serving in the church and not just going to church was going to make me more accountable. It was going to make me stronger in Christ because you couldn't just be on a ministry at church living any kind of way. One question they asked, and this is not verbatim, was about the type of relationship I was in. I was super proud to be able to say that I was not in any relationship, although I knew God was still delivering me.

The first song that I mimed to was "All I Have to Give" by Mali Music. It was the chorus of the song that just messed me all the way up. The chorus went like this:

> Here is my heart, my mind
> Lord, here's my life
> My everything
> Take it
> It's yours, oh Lord
> It's all I have to give

This part broke me down, but in a good way. It made me surrender a lot more to Him. I can't say that I surrendered all the way, but I can say that what I did give took some pressure off of me and made me stronger.

STANDING OUT from the CROWD

Little did I know that serving God would be the thing that separated me from the crowd. My elevation in ministry was becoming my separation from the world. The Bible tells us in 2 Corinthians 5:17 (GW translation) that whoever is a believer in Christ is a new creation. The old way of living has **disappeared**. **A new** way of living has come into **existence**. I was starting to see God's word being manifested in my life. My new way of living would be to get a more personal relationship with God and not worry so much about the people and things that I felt I was losing because of it.

Regarding my old life, one thing I was feeling led to do was to change the way I dressed. It was not that I felt like I had to or because it was the correct thing to do; what you wear is the least of how God sees you. It was not because I wanted men to start looking at me differently because I still was not interested in dating. For me, it was more about the fact that the clothes seemed to define part of who I thought I was for so many years. Shopping in the men's section for jeans, boxers, and button-ups, I was still associating myself with the "male role." I felt boyish, and I wondered how I was ever going to get delivered from this if I couldn't even get "out of character"? I was out one time by myself mainly because I did not want to be around anybody, and I was working on being single, but while I was out by myself, a man approached me. He was an older guy in his late forties or early fifties, but he started a conversation with me because he was interested in me. I engaged in the conversation with him because that's just what I do and who I am, but he said something to me that made me think about the way I dressed.

Him: "You dating anybody?"

Me: "No."

Him: "Why not?"

Me: "Because I am in a transitioning stage of my life."

Him: "What does that mean?"

Me: "I used to date girls, but God is delivering me from that."

Him: Okay, nothing wrong with that. I wouldn't have been able to tell with what you're wearing."

Me: "Is it the hat?"

Our conversation goes on a little longer, and then he leaves. The next morning, that word just sat with me, and I started to be more conscious about the way I was dressing. I was changing on the inside, but I felt it needed to begin to show on the outside. On June 6, 2017, I would take another outward step to show that I wanted to be what Christ created me to be. My cross would get a little heavy as I went through my closet and got rid of mostly all the men's clothing and accessories that I had, from hoodies to sweaters to jeans to collared shirts to polo shirts to swim trunks, boxers, men's cologne, men's watches, you name it; if it was male-related; I packed it up. I cried while I was doing it. I had worship music on while I was doing it. I kept telling myself and the Holy Spirit kept telling me it's worth it. "I am going to restore all of these things back to you one hundredfold. Your faith is making you whole, and I received it."

My pastor caught wind of what I had done, and he explained to me that God sees our heart, not so much the outward appearance and that doing that was not necessarily a mandate from God, but he was proud of me for taking that step. When you make room for God, he makes ways for you. Not even a week later, my mom blessed me with a gift card to a clothing store in order to purchase women's clothing for myself. I hardly wore regular clothes during that time anyway because I was a PE teacher, and basketball season is year-round, so basketball gear was my go-to, yet it was just enough to purchase a few pair of jeans and a few shirts from the women's section to get me started in case I did go somewhere and especially when I went to church on Sunday.

What had I gotten myself into? I mean, I knew I was going to wear the clothes, but did I stop and think about how uncomfortable I would be in them? What my "homeboys" (girl best friends) were going to think about this "new" look? Nope, I only thought about what I was trying to do for God—to please Him in any way. Once again, God honored my outward demonstration of wanting Him to be a part of my life by surrounding me with people who did not persecute me but praised me. Now don't get me wrong; my friends definitely joked, but they waited a few weeks to do it, LOL. I would have done the same thing with them, so it was all good! They welcomed me with open arms, expressed how proud they were of me, and respected my decision to follow God.

One of them did question why I had to change the way I dressed because they couldn't see themselves doing that if they were to ever leave the lifestyle. But I explained to them what I explained to you. I also explained to her that we all have our own routes when it comes to deliverance, even if it is the same type of deliverance. So it was nothing that she had to do per se because God meets us right where we are. This was the path that I could handle, so I took this route.

My pastor would also make it his business to tell me how beautiful I was, and he mentioned that it was important for him to say that to me as my father in the faith so that I could hear it from a male. It's like how a father should demonstrate to his daughter how she should be treated by another male. That blessed me so much that he thought about me enough to make sure I felt good about what I was doing.

Their encouragement helped me to feel more comfortable in my "skin" and new clothes. The saying "God works in mysterious ways" is not just a cliché; God works things out so smoothly, you don't even notice the difference. What I mean is that, while I was working on dressing differently, God allowed about three events to happen where I had to wear female clothing. Other than the fact that people were not used to seeing me in that type of clothing, it was still expected because of the occasion.

The first event that happened was me babysitting and taking the kids to the pool. The kids I was babysitting (my nieces, nephew, and a long-time friend's kids) had never seen me in a bathing suit, so I wondered how they would take it. As the saying goes, "Kids say the darndest things," so I was afraid of what they might say. Their body language was a message in itself when they looked confused and had big eyes as if they had never seen me before, LOL.

"Auntie Kara, you have on a bathing suit?"

LOL um, yes, we are going to the pool, right? I had one of them take a picture of me that I eventually would post on IG with the caption "The new me is really still the old me" (Drake). I was starting to become whom God was calling me to be all along, and although my appearance looked different, I was still Kara. I got the most likes I had ever gotten on any picture that I posted and about forty-five comments that were so uplifting and encouraging. God used that moment to spread his love through other people so that I would become even more comfortable with who He was molding me into.

Next would be my cousin's wedding. I wore a dress for the first time in a long time, but because it was appropriate to be in a dress for the wedding, I was not as uncomfortable. The compliments I received from my family, especially the ones I had not seen in years, gave me more encouragement. I also posted a picture of me in the dress on IG and got a lot more encouraging compliments. Please hear me when I say this: I was **not** looking for the approval of people when I posted any of those pictures. Yet I was showing the world another outward appearance of my commitment to Christ, and He softened those people's hearts to receive Him and what He was doing on the inside and outside of me.

The third event that took place was a mini vacation I took by myself. I stayed with a close friend of mine who is a male, and I was in a new environment where he was the only person who knew the "old me." We went to a few places to eat and hang out, which meant I would be in public with "women's clothes" on. Clothes such as heels, a shirt that would show my stomach and shoulders, sandals, and fitted jeans. Clothes that I had picked out all by myself and wanted to wear, especially since I was going to be around "new" people. Even in my male clothes, I did my best to look my best, and I needed to feel comfortable in the outfit that I was rocking. It would be no different once I began to wear women's clothing. I saw it as a great time to practice my new style. If I could be comfortable around people who knew me, I could surely be comfortable around people who didn't know me.

Even with all the encouragement and me showing the world that I was okay with who I was becoming, I learned very soon that what I wore had nothing to do with who I was because girls were still attracted to me and trying to get entangled with me. There was way more to this journey of carrying my cross than just changing the way I dressed, which I knew it would be, but this still was a start for me.

I remember being in church, and the elder was speaking about how his life had changed. There was a particular time when he saw his old friends, and they called him by his nickname when he was out in the world. He immediately corrected his friends because he knew that that nickname was a reference to his old self. When he and his friends would hear that name, they expected that person, but he was no longer that person. I've said this before, but it fits this part of my story as well: "The name of a thing reveals the nature of a thing" (Dr. Magee). KJ was my "boy" name; it was my name when I was gay. It was my name that meant I was not Kara, to most people anyway. Some people genuinely called me KJ because those are my initials, but even then, I knew the difference.

The revelation I received from this word would begin to convict me, and I felt led to do something about it. I made up my mind that from now on, if I was asked my name, it was either Kara, K, or Coach K. I was no longer KJ to anybody. If someone called me that, and I knew they were referring to the "boy" version of me, I would have to correct them, and I may be making that sound easy, but it was not. The enemy made me feel like I was acting bougie or being too good for people now because I wanted them to call me Kara, K, or Coach K. But I had to deny the enemy and realize this was part of my deliverance process and not allow him to keep me from that. It took a couple of times for me to adjust to what I was working on doing, but when I got the hang of it, God gave me peace about it, and yet another weight had lifted off of me. Just in case you missed what I was saying, remember the part in *Coming to America* when they were debating calling Muhammad Ali by his birth name or his new name, and I quote, "His mama named Clay imma call him Clay." Therefore, my momma named me Kara. You can call me Kara, and the only nicknames I answer to are K and Coach K.

People were starting to see me differently, and I was starting to see myself differently. I was growing apart from this footpath of a lifestyle I had created for myself and beginning to walk the path God had for me, and it felt good. Not as many females were approaching me, and I was looking the other way as much as I had the strength to.

Standing out from the crowd didn't mean that I was better than anyone; it didn't mean that I was being noticed by everyone. It just simply meant what the word of God tells us in Romans 8:12–14 (MSG): "So don't you see that we don't owe this old do-it-yourself life one red cent. There's nothing in it for us, nothing at all. The best thing to do is give it a decent burial and get on with your new life. God's Spirit beckons. There are things to do and places to go!"

UNexpected GIFTS

"The more that you read, the more things you will know. The more that you learn, the more places you will go" (*Dr. Seuss*, a childhood book with an adulthood message). I was never a big reader; in fact, I only read directions, instructions, short documents, and things of that sort, but books were out of the question. When it came to school, I only lasted because I was playing basketball, and I knew I needed the grades to play. I vowed to never go back to school once I graduated from college, which should give you somewhat of an understanding of my relationship with reading and learning.

People would give me books, mainly about coaching, but I would start them and then never finish. My journey to reading would begin in my walk with God. The relationship I talked about in the chapter "Strength" caused me to dive into God's word every single day. I was reading devotion after devotion, scripture after scripture, sometimes three devotions at a time—when I woke up in the morning, when I went to bed at night, if I couldn't sleep through the night, or if I was just in a slump—**I was reading**.

In my reading, I found out so much about myself, my circumstances, and my God. Additionally, I started to appreciate reading so much that the next thing I knew, I was buying a book from our church bookstore titled *The Purpose of Living* by Nate Holcomb. The book talked about how to be a better steward of my life; it showed me what God needed from me and what He would do to help me in the process. The next book I read was called *From Point Guard to Prophet* by Sophia Ruffin. In her book, God showed me, **me**. I saw myself in the entire book—from her struggle with homosexuality to her feelings of rejection, torment, and abandonment, and to her relationship with God. After reading that book, I knew I was on the right track. That book freed me; it showed me how loving God really is. It allowed me to not be ashamed that even though I was not completely delivered from homosexuality, I could still be who God was calling me to be. I began to share books that I was reading with other people, and as a result, people were giving me more books.

In addition to reading more books, God spoke to me and kindly told me that I had to go back to school, as if appreciating reading was not enough. I'm like, "God, you're just going to disregard the fact that I vowed not to ever go back to school?"

God's response: "My ways are higher than your ways… I know the plans for your life, and they are plans to prosper you."

My response: "If you say so, Lord," shaking my head.

This would not only be a challenge because I had no desire to ever go back to school, but at the time, I was working three jobs, which meant I was going to have to take online classes (which I felt would be a struggle for me because I am a hands-on learner). I didn't have a computer of my own at home, and I definitely didn't have the money to pay for school. I had no clue about the major I was about to take on; my bachelor's degree is in physical education, and now I would begin to pursue my associate's degree in **business**.

> ## When God tells you to do something, He makes a way for you to do it.

When God tells you to do something, He makes a way for you to do it. I was not aware of some of the benefits I had being an employee at the college I was coaching for until one day I was speaking with the head coach, and he mentioned that his sister was attending the college for free because it was part of an employee's contract for some family members to attend school for free, including the employee themselves. And there goes my excuse for "I don't have the money to pay for school." For we know that **all things** work together for the good of those who love HIM (Romans 8:28). There were some fees that I had to pay, but God provided that every time I needed it as well. I did my research, got the paperwork in, and signed up for school. I started out part-time just to test my ability to manage my time and do an online class. God helped me to do well so after that semester, I became a full-time student, which meant I was taking two classes at a time.

Next thing you know, I went to a business meeting where we were looking to build a gym for the college. The place we met was an old school that had shut down and was bought out by another staff member. As we were walking through the building, we stopped through the library, and there were tons of computers. They were old but they worked. The person we were meeting with was like, "If you know anybody looking for a computer, I'm giving these away." In my mind, my brain cells were doing flips and going crazy. Like, "This cannot be happening right now," but it was. I opened my mouth and said, "For real, because I need one."

His words: "It's yours."

On the way home, I couldn't do anything but laugh and thank God. I had to get some work done for the computer to work properly, but I believe that was just a test to see if I really trusted that this was God's plan for me. I set up a nice little work center in my apartment, and I took my first online course. God saw that I was being obedient with what I had, so He blessed me with a brand-new laptop—purchased by the one and only, my **mom**! With me traveling during basketball season, it would have been a lot harder to get work done on the road without one.

So far, God has given me the time to manage online classes, the finances to pay for school, and the tools I needed to be successful in school. Now, how was He going to turn this brain of mine to learn a completely different career? Well, let's start with how I didn't realize it then, but I know now that He had prepared me for this all along.

One of the three jobs I had at the time was being a sailing instructor. There was a program the school joined a few years before that offered sailing courses as a PE credit for middle school–aged children. They eventually made it a health and PE credit, which is where I came in. I would teach the kids health for an hour, and then they would sail for an hour and a half. Long story short, the staff thought I would be helpful doing summer camp, and for some extra money, I said, "Why not?" Although I was not familiar with marine biology and sailing, I learned quite a bit that summer, including how to sail a Harbor 20. I said all this to say that God had already exercised my strength to learn a completely new subject.

I completed my associate of business degree on June 22, 2020; I worked willingly at completing school, and I did it as if I was doing it for the Lord (Colossians 3:23), which I was because I definitely didn't ask to be back in school. Because of that, I graduated with honors for the first time in my life and made the dean's list every semester; when God is in it, there is no **limit**.

The title of this chapter is "Unexpected Gift." The word **unexpected** means not expected or regarded as likely to happen (Webster's Dictionary). Some synonyms for unexpected are unanticipated, unforeseen, and unpredicted. I simply went to school because I was committed to being obedient to God, and He told me to go back to school. Where business came from, I had no idea.

I began school in October 2018, and in June 2019, I started a business called Prep Camp Academy. A parent and old schoolmate called me to see if I could get her into our gym for her daughter's basketball team to practice. While talking to her, something said (God told me) to ask if her daughters needed a personal trainer, so I asked (being obedient), and she said yes. Isaiah 1:19 (MEV) says, "If you are willing and obedient, you will eat the good of the land." Not only did I train her two daughters, but she referred me to some of her daughters' teammates, and they wanted to get training as well. The class that I was in at the time was called Marketing Principles, and it could not have come at a better time. I needed to know how to get my name out there and market my business, and that is exactly what the class was about.

The book I was reading at the time, *God Is My CEO* by Larry Julian, was teaching me to run my business in a Christlike manner. It taught me how to stand firm on God's principles and not give in to the business principles that society shows us. A former student of mine was finishing her master's at ODU as a graphic designer, and she designed the logo for me. A good friend of mine was in the T-shirt business, and he screen-printed shirts for me. Another good friend of mine had a lot of time off from work and was able to be my assistant, and she helped me with my schoolwork, might I add. I was eating the **good of the land; everything was working together for my good**!

There were some challenges along the way. For example, I put out flyers to host summer camp for a total of five weeks, but only two people signed up. I didn't allow that to discourage me, however, because I was learning to put my trust in the Lord. If He gave me the business, everything was going to work at the right time.

In March of 2020, the next challenge that would hit my business would be COVID-19. The gym I was using was the school that I was working from, which God gave me favor with because I resigned in the 2018–2019 school year because God told me to, COVID-19 caused the building to close, and as I am writing this book (September 2020), it is still not open. The business was at a halt, but God will generously provide all you need. Then you will always have everything you need and plenty left over to share with others (2 Corinthians 9:8 NLT).

Because we are made in Christ's image and likeness, we have to do things that we dread, just as He had to do something He dreaded. I am not a fan of training outside, and I like to be close and personal with my clients, so virtual and outside workouts were not on my list of things to do. However, if you are faithful over a few things, God will make you ruler over many things (Matthew 25:23). In June of 2020, I took my talents outside, and God blessed me with new clients, **unexpected gifts**, and brought back some of the old ones. In August of 2020, the same phone call I received to ask if I had a gym her daughters' team could use was the same person who called me to say, "I have a gym you can use." **Unexpected gifts**! I was in the gym the following week, and since then, I've had five more new clients. **Unexpected gifts**! This has yet to happen, but I am going to speak it into existence: I will own my **own gym**.

If you are in college right now, have ever been to college, and/or have majored in business, then you know that for that year and a half I was writing, researching, doing Albert Einstein math, more writing and researching, project after project, and more writing and researching.

What I didn't **expect** was that it would lead me to write my first book. Remember when I said that reading was my least favorite thing to do? Well, writing was probably my second least favorite thing to do. So much so that the one time I got ISS in high school was because my English teacher didn't give me the grade I thought I deserved for a paper I did, so I called her a stupid jerk and walked out of the classroom. Lord, if I haven't asked for forgiveness for that, please forgive me.

God: "Forgiven!"

Okay, as I was saying, I never would have imagined writing a book, being an author, but I'm sure God saw this coming the whole time. Like what in the world was I going to write about? In the process of me giving up my lifestyle, I started a series on Instagram called "BIGGER than ME." On the series, I talked about my struggle with breaking away from the relationship I was in. I cried, I laughed, I talked about it every Monday. I was transparent, I told the good, the bad, and the ugly, and more importantly, I told the **truth**. I would get direct messages from people who were following me saying they were encouraged by what I was doing, they were struggling too and didn't know how to deal with it, and they would cry with me and encourage me to keep going. I honestly was not doing it for anybody else; I was doing it for myself. It was my way of being accountable and sticking to what God was dealing with me about. It was **BIGGER than ME** because my lifestyle change was no longer about me; it was no longer I who lived but it was the Christ that was living inside of me (Galatians 2:20).

As time went on, God spoke a word to my mom, and He had spoken it to me as well, but I didn't realize that I was hearing from God at the time. God told her and me that the name of my first book would be **BIGGER than ME**. Needless to say, where was the lie? However, this book is not just to demonstrate the Christ that is living inside of me as being **BIGGER than ME**, but it's **BIGGER than ME** because so many people like me need to hear my story. They need to know that even though they struggle with homosexuality, God still loves them and nothing can separate them from God's love. They need to know that God will meet them right where they are with open arms. They need to know that God will begin to do a new thing in them if they would just allow Him to. They need to know that God sees them so much differently than how anybody else, including themselves, may see them. They need to know that God can and He will deliver, save, and set free anyone, including **them**. They need to know that there is no condemnation in Christ Jesus.

My story is my cross; it's my crucifixion. It's the image of God in me that laid down His life for all of us to be saved, and now I have laid down my lifestyle in order for other people to be saved by God. I surrendered all to God for myself and for anybody else who is struggling with believing that homosexuality, lesbianism, or gay is just who they are. Everyone who is in Christ becomes a **new** creature; the **old** way of living is **gone**, and the **new** way of living has **begun** (2 Corinthians 5:17). My life is **BIGGER than ME** because it's not about me, but it's all about bringing glory to God here on earth by doing the things He created me to do (John 17:4).

Learning to Lead like Jesus: 11 Principles to Help You Serve, Inspire, & Equip Others by Boyd Bailey gave me confirmation that this was all in God's plan. I am here to serve, inspire, and equip others, which sounds about right based on the **unexpected gifts** of Prep Camp Academy and **BIGGER than ME.**

The End is really the BEginNIng

Seventeen years of living a lifestyle of homosexuality and two years of living my life for Christ does not equal deliverance. Now don't get me wrong, if God wanted to just instantly set me free from homosexuality, I do not doubt for one second that He could, but I do believe that He has not because there is a lot that I need to learn about myself and Him. I believe He knows that everyone I share my story with will need to see that God loves them and wants to be in a relationship with them **just the way they are.** He wants to show the believers and nonbelievers that they do not have to "get their lives together" before coming to Him. More importantly, they can't get their lives together without Him.

I believe my story will also help the Christian reading this, who ridicules the LGBQIA+ community, to see Christ for who He really is, and that is the **Savior of the LOST.** The truth is that my story is by far over. I still struggle with feelings for another female even in the midst of writing this book. I've gone back and forth with God, myself, and her. One day my flesh wins and I'm intimate with her. Another day my spirit wins, and I fight off the feelings I have for her.

Remember what I said earlier about temptation: if the desire is in you the enemy can and will tempt you with it, but God will always give you an outlet. I had to realize that this spirit was still in me, and I had to start recognizing the outlets **daily.** Second Corinthians 12:9 says, "My grace (Jesus talking) is all you need, My power works best in weakness, and I knew I was in a very weak stage of my life." The word **weak** in the scripture means inability. The Lord declares to

Paul and also to me that His empowerment (grace) is optimized in situations that are beyond our natural ability.

So although I am taking steps in the right direction by walking with Christ, constantly reading my word, praying, attending Church regularly, and feeding my spirit with Christlike things as much as possible, the Lord's grace is what is going to get me through this thing. This would have to be an **everyday decision** on my part to allow God to do just that and not get caught up in trying to use "my own power" to get me through. Every day I'm asking God to help me, to forgive me, to strengthen me, and to get me through this, and I believe that He is doing exactly that.

I told the woman I had feelings for that the only time I am going to hurt her is when I walk completely away from this lifestyle. When I said that to her, it felt like it had already happened, like I was speaking to that homosexual spirit in faith that I am going to be delivered from this once and for all one day. I know the Lord placed this woman in my life. We started out as friends. She was praying with me and for me, talking me through a rough day with God's word, something my other friends weren't able to do at the time. She gave me someone I could call when I didn't want to be by myself. She had her own things going on as well, which I felt like I could help her with by using God's word just as she was helping me. The enemy had other plans and not being aware of how vulnerable we both were at the time, we allowed the enemy to pervert our friendship. Let me insert this here: the enemy has many costumes, and he knows our patterns better than we do. He also knows the word of God, so be aware of situations like mine, and do your best to snap out of it and see things through God's eyes.

I had a lot of mixed feelings such as, I was letting God down again, I was letting myself down again, people would think I was a hypocrite, and I thought I was past this stage, but I realized this, too, was the enemy trying to get me to give up on what I had decided in my heart to do, which was to be delivered from homosexuality. I had personally been here before, letting go of an ungodly relationship in order to walk in the purpose God had for me, so I knew I could better handle letting go of the relationship we made it to be, in order to get back the relationship God called it to be. The end was deciding to be delivered from homosexuality, the beginning was choosing each day to allow God to deliver me. **Bigger than me** was the end; bigger than **us** would be my new beginning. "**God's grace empowers us to go beyond our natural ability.**"

> "**God's grace empowers us to go beyond our natural ability.**"

Devotional

Day 1

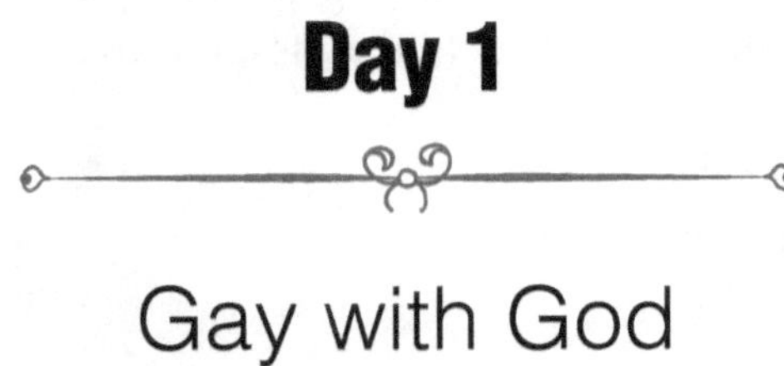

Gay with God

Today, I want to introduce this devotion and give you clarity on what "gay with God" means. This devotion is inspired by my book, *Bigger than Me*, which goes into why I engaged in the homosexual lifestyle, the struggles I had with the lifestyle, and how God has delivered me from homosexuality. In John 17:4, the Bible says that I will bring glory to your name here on earth by completing the things you've called me to do. The two reasons for writing the book and this devotion is simply because I was called to do it, and it will bring glory to God's name by spreading the word of God to the LGBQIA+ community and others in love.

Gay with God is a play on words and does not mean that God approves of homosexuality, as I go into detail later in this devotion. Instead, gay with God means that contrary to what most people believe, God desires a relationship with you even if you are gay. Scripture clearly tells us that even in our sins, Christ died for all of us (Romans 5:8). Think about it, would you cut your hair before going to get a haircut? Or would you wait until you felt better before going to the doctor? Then my question to you is, why do we believe we must wait to get our life together before coming to Christ? Hence, the title of the devotion, "Gay with God." It could have been "Depressed with God," "Drug Addict with God," or "Fornicator with God," yet I can only tell you my story and how I was once gay with God until He turned my life around.

I pray that this devotion draws more of the LGBQIA+ community to Christ and informs the religious people who have pushed many in the LGBQIA+ community away that through Jesus, our sins are forgiven and not only sins that are "acceptable" to society but those of the **whole world**, which includes homosexuals (1 John 2:2).

- John 17:4
- Romans 5:8
- 1 John 2:2

Day 2

Root Cover-Up

Molested, no father figure in my life, and my mother never showing me affection—these are all reasons that I believed led me to choose the homosexual lifestyle.

Being raised in the church, whether you want to be there or not, you hear things that may not make sense right then, but eventually, a light bulb comes on. I've always heard this particular scripture but never paid attention to it: Psalm 51:1 (NLT): "For I was born a sinner—yes, from the moment my mother conceived me." What! **We were all born sinners**? So was this God's plan all along? The Bible never says which sin; it just says **sin**. Contrary to what you might believe, sin is sin; there is no big sin or small sin, and there is no one sin that God accepts more than another sin. We sometimes hear the LGBQIA+ community say that they were born this way, and although I do not agree with the motive behind saying that, as if it were a genetic thing, I cannot skip over the fact that the root of liking girls has been **covered** up. Yes, the things I mentioned earlier happened to me and added fuel to the fire; however, the bottom line reason was that because of Adam and Eve's downfall, I was born into sin, even though it was one that I chose to nourish.

It was important for me to begin with what I believe are the roots of my homosexual lifestyle choice, not to make an excuse or blame anyone, but so that you understand I do not regret who I was. I do not condemn myself or anyone else who has been or is a part of the LGBQIA+ community. I am so far from perfect while even writing this devotion, but I understand that it is now part of my purpose in life to face my truths and share my journey because it's **BIGGER than ME**. My pastor says, in order to be delivered from any situation, you must "face it, trace it, and then you can erase it" (Apostle Johnny L. Magee Jr.). My heart, as you continue to read, is for you to be able to face your truths and trace your roots, and together we both can continue to be delivered by God and get closer to Him. "He that the Son has set free is free indeed" (John 8:36)! To God be the glory!

- Psalm 51:1
- Genesis 3:16–23
- John 8:36

Day 3

Lifestyle

The more I hung out with my teammate, I began to pick up on the way she acted and dressed. Her pants and shirt were big, a little saggy, and her voice was deeper than most girls, at least the ones I knew. I also started to notice other people on the team who acted and dressed like her too. From an outsider's perspective, they seemed to be having fun all the time, many people knew them, and they felt loved—exactly what high school was supposed to be like, right? This could be the last time you ever hear me say this: I wanted to be like them. I tested the waters and got myself a girlfriend. Now I had to change the way I talked, dressed, and acted, right? I was still in the closet (hiding my sexuality), so if I changed the way I dressed or acted, people would surely notice and begin to label me. Little did I know, people were already labeling me because everyone but me could see that I was changing. My best friend looked, dressed, and carried herself like a boy. I began to buy men's sneakers and then an outfit from the men's section to go with the sneakers. My clothes were bought big because that's how my teammates and best friend were wearing their clothes. I still had most of my girl clothes though because I still had to go to church and whatever church functions, but at school and at work, you better believe I had on my "boy" clothes. I wanted to show that I was gay so that the girls would approach me.

I'm sure if you have ever been a part of the LGBQIA+ community, you are familiar with this part of my story. I brought this particular section out of the book to show you the real reason why God does not approve of the homosexual lifestyle. Simply put, it was not God's **design**. As I would sit in church while being in the life-style, I would always be waiting for the day our pastor would speak on homosexuality. I wondered how I would feel when he finally did, but to my surprise, when he finally spoke on the topic, I was not offended at all. I was more enlightened about why God did not approve of homosexuality, and all the critics were **wrong**. He actually started the message by congratulating the LGBQIA+ community for gaining their civil rights (this is when the Supreme Court approved gay marriage). The title of his message was "The Supreme Court has ruled and God has not changed His mind."

- 2 Timothy 3:16
- Daniel 6:1–15

Day 4

God's Design

This is not a bashing session on the LGBQIA+ community. This is to **inform** those who are "gay with God" (meaning you are a part of the LGBQIA+ community, you're saved, and have a relationship with God) and those who aren't aware of why God does not approve of the homosexual lifestyle and what the **Bible** says about living this type of lifestyle. Based on what my pastor ministered on that day, here are three reasons why God is not for same-sex relationships/ marriage:

1. It goes against God's intended **protocol** (order) (Genesis 2:18–22). God created male and female in that order. Notice how I went from wearing female clothes to wearing male clothes in my book. Notice I mentioned how my friends at the time were taking on male characteristics: deep voices, clothing, and oftentimes male haircuts or hairstyles. What I have experienced when being in the lifestyle is that there is often a dominant person in the relationship (usually the masculine role) and a nondominant person in the relationship (usually the feminine role).
2. It goes against God's intended **purpose**. God's intended purpose is to procreate so we can populate (Genesis 1:27). When same-sex couples want to have a child, they cannot

do it "naturally," or between the two of them when being sexually active with each other.

3. It goes against God's intended **pleasure**. Sexual intercourse was designed by God specifically for males and females (Romans 1:26–27).

- 2 Timothy 3:16
- Genesis 2:18–22
- Genesis 1:27
- Romans 1:26–27

Day 5

Inside Her World

I definitely was no saint, and the only future I saw myself having was being with girls because that's who I had become. The problem with that was that it was not the way God intended for me to be loved. There is something in all of us called conviction, and it was something that I experienced every now and then when I was in college and even more after college. I remember dating one girl on the basketball team, and we would go to her aunt's house sometimes on the weekend. That did not last long because her aunt was a Christian, and she figured out that we were in a relationship. So she did what everyone else did and threatened to cut her niece off if she did not stop dating me, so we had to end our relationship. I think this forced me to go back to church, and I remember getting baptized shortly after and doing my best to not like girls anymore. To no surprise, going cold turkey when deciding not to be gay anymore is not quite the way it works. At the time, I did not understand that God was not asking for my sexuality more than He was asking for me to enter into a relationship with Him.

My heart for this devotion and my book **Bigger than Me** is to show everyone, especially the LGBQIA+ community, that you can be "gay with God." We fail to realize that we all sin and fall short of God's glorious standards, and being homosexual is simply a sin. God will meet us where we are. The Bible is clear when it says in Romans 8: 38-39, "**Nothing** can **separate us** (you or me) from the love of God," which, to me, means He will accept you gay, a liar, a thief, or whatever your sin(s) are. So many times, religious Christians push the LGBQIA+ community away because it is not God's design. However, God is not about religion; He is about relationships, and He wants us in a relationship with Him to **save** us from our sins.

- Romans 3:23
- Romans 8:38–39
- Luke 19:10

Day 6

Strength

God was dealing with me so heavily that night. I was so scared because I knew the time had come when I was really going to put my love for God to the test. I remember calling her and trying to sound normal, but my voice kept crackling. She eventually asked the question I did not want to answer. "What's wrong?" It was like a fifteen-second pause from me and then a deep sigh. As I began to tell her that God was dealing with me about our relationship, the tears just started to flow. I honestly don't know how she heard a word I said because I couldn't stop crying, and then she was crying. I told her that God was dealing with me and that we were not going to be able to continue our relationship. I told her I didn't know what to do. I wanted to get baptized because I wanted to be serious with Christ, and I didn't feel that God was pleased with the fact that she was the only reason why I was not going to get baptized. My actions toward her were different in those few months anyway because I was doing what I thought was my best to work on "not being gay."

I've learned that in any relationship, there is a hidden expectation of change between both people. Just like Christ, we a lot of times (Christ does it all the time) accept people just the way they are. We may not like the fact that they smoke, curse, are not currently working, or have their own apartment, but we still decide to be in a relationship with them, and at the same time, we anticipate that those things will change eventually. We don't go into the relationship trying to change them; we just hope that he or she will love us enough to stop doing those things, especially when they know we aren't fond of it. I would submit to you that this is the same way it is when we are in a relationship with Christ. The Bible clearly states, "When we are in Christ we are **new** (changed) creatures, the old life is gone and a **new** life has begun" (2 Corinthians 5:17), which, to me, means it is impossible to stay the same when you have a relationship with Him. So yes, God is love, and yes, He loves everyone the way they are, but His love is not what's in question. The question is how much do you love Him back? Jackie Hill Perry said it best: "Lord, help us to love you more than we love our sins."

Being in a relationship with Christ is the only way He can save us from our sins and make our lives new, which is why Satan wants to keep you out of a relationship with Christ.

- Matthew 16:24–25
- 2 Corinthians 5:17
- Luke 9:23–24

Day 7

Standing Out from the Crowd

KJ was my "boy" name; it was my name when I was gay. It was the name that meant I was not Kara, at least to most people. Some people genuinely called me KJ because those are my initials, but even then, I knew the difference. The revelation I received from this word would begin to convict me, and I felt led to do something about it. I made up my mind that from now on, if I was asked my name, it would either be Kara, K, or Coach K. I would no longer be KJ to anybody. If someone called me that and I knew they were referring to the "boy" version of me, I would have to correct them. I may be making that sound easy, but it was not. The enemy made me feel like I was acting bougie or being too good for people now because I wanted them to call me Kara, K, or Coach K. But I had to deny the enemy and realize this was part of my deliverance process and not allow him to keep me from that. It took a couple of times for me to adjust to what I was working on doing, but when I got the hang of it, God gave me peace about it, and yet another weight had lifted off of me.

Romans 12:2 (ERV) says, "Don't change yourselves to be like the people of this world, but let God change you inside with a new way of thinking. Then you will be able to understand and accept what God wants for you." The first thing you will have to do when standing out from the crowd is change the way you think. You will have to separate yourself from the things that trigger you to go back to your old ways. Ask an alcoholic or drug addict how hard it is to stay clean if they still go to parties where "friends" are doing drugs and alcohol. My path was referring to myself by my first name and changing the way I dressed because I thought the clothes and name were my identity to the lifestyle. Your path may be different, but whatever it is, you will not be able to do the things you used to do, talk the way you used to talk, go to places that you used to go, and hang out with some people you used to hang out with if you are going to stand out from the crowd. God will give you the desire and power to do what pleases Him (Philippians 2:13)! Be **encouraged**!

- Romans 8:5–6
- Romans 12:2
- 1 Peter 1:13
- Philippians 2:13

Day 8

Prayer

In my time of transitioning, I found a few prayers that I would read every morning in faith that I felt got me through my roughest times because I didn't feel like I knew how to pray or even what to pray. I have gotten a little better at knowing how to pray and what to pray for, so I wanted to leave this prayer for you. Pray this prayer every day if you remember, and even if you don't, pray this prayer when you know you need to but can't find the words.

Prayer

Father, first and foremost, thank you for another day. Thank you for allowing me another chance to get things right. Thank you for your grace and new mercies that you grant me each day to walk upright before you. Thank you for loving me just the way I am. Thank you for meeting me where I am.

Thank you, Lord, for being so patient with me, as your word says in Peter 3:9, "The Lord is not slow to fulfill his promise as some count slowness, but is patient toward you, not wishing that any should perish, but that all should reach repentance."

Father, please forgive me for my sins. Forgive me for those things that I do that are not pleasing to you. Lord, help me to love you more than I love my sins. Convict my spirit when I am doing things that are not pleasing to you. First Corinthians 10:13 says that you will not allow the temptation to be more than I can stand and that you will show me a way out so that I can endure. Lord, please help me to be aware of the outlets you give me when the temptations of life come.

Lord, I am asking for peace at this time of my life. Peace that surpasses all of my understanding. Peace when I am choosing to please you and not the world. Peace when I am choosing to please you and not myself. Peace when you begin to protect me and remove people from my life who are no longer for me. Peace when I feel like it's just me and I'm all alone. Your word says that you will never leave me or forsake me (Hebrews 13:5), and I believe your word.

Lord, I am asking for strength, your strength that says I can do all things through Christ who strengthens me (Philippians 4:13). Strength when I am discouraged, strength not to look back, strength to run and not be weary, strength to walk and not faint in the name of Jesus.

Father, you said that faith comes by hearing and hearing the word of God (Romans 10:17). Lord, remind me of your word when I struggle with my faith in getting through this transition. Remind me that you will give me the desire and power to do what pleases you (Philippians 2:13). Remind me that I am loved by you (Romans 5:8). Remind me to trust in you with all my heart and lean not on my understanding (Proverbs 3:5). Remind me not to get weary in well-doing because you have a harvest for me in the end (Galatians 6:9). You said that you are close to the brokenhearted (Psalms 34:18), so Father, continue to draw close to me as I draw close to you.

Lord, I am hurting, this is hard, I don't know if I can do this, I am weak, I love her/him, I feel like I can't be without them. Lord, I boast in my weakness so that your power can rest upon me (2 Corinthians 12:9). The same power that raised you from the dead is living inside of me and will raise me from the dead too. I am a new creature in you; old things have passed away, and all things have become new (2 Corinthians 5:17). I will not be conformed to the patterns of this world but rather I will be transformed by the renewing of my mind (Romans 12:2). It is in Jesus's name that I seal this prayer. Amen. Amen.

- John 14:13

About the Author

Kara Jackson, affectionately known as Coach K, is a lover of teaching. Whether it is in the form of coaching, training, or teaching God's word, Kara has a way of breaking down information in a way many people can receive. Kara was a health and PE teacher for twelve years until she heard God say it was time to move on to an assistant coach for women's basketball. As a teacher and a coach her, connection to her students and players wasn't just about health, PE, and basketball, but also pouring into them what God has poured into her. Because of what God has done in her life, Kara has been led to share through her writing what He has done for her and what He will also do for you. Kara loves the Lord and her gifts of service, evangelism, shepherding, and teaching. She is the daughter of John Jackson and Deborah Amin, the twin sister of Kelli Fairbanks, and the younger sister of Sherisse Kenerson and Sarel Jackson, who are also twins.

Colossians 3:17: "And whatever you do or say, do it as a representative of the Lord Jesus, giving thanks through him to God the Father."